Living with a Brother or Sister with Special Needs

Living with a Brother or Sister with Special Needs

A Book for Sibs

by Donald Meyer and Patricia Vadasy

Foreword by Thomas H. Powell
Drawings by R. Scott Vance

Second Edition, Revised and Expanded

University of Washington Press Seattle and London

Library of Congress Cataloging-in-Publication Data

Meyer, Donald J. (Donald Joseph), 1951-
    Living with a Brother or Sister with special needs : a book for sibs / by Donald Meyer and Patricia Vadasy ; foreword by Thomas H. Powell ; drawings by R. Scott Vance. — 2nd ed., rev. and expanded.
        p.   cm.
    Includes bibliographical references and index.
    ISBN 0-295-97547-4 (alk. paper)
    1. Handicapped children—Family relationships.   2. Handicapped children—Home care.   3. Brothers and Sisters.   I. Vadasy, Patricia F.   II. Title.
HV888.M49   1996
362.4'043—dc20   96-7020
                                                                                   CIP

The paper used in this publication meets the minimum requirements of American National Standard for Information Sciences–Permanence of Paper for Printed Library Materials, ANSI Z39. 48-1984. ∞

Contents

Foreword

When Cate was born, she came into the world in the usual way, surrounded by joyful parents, brothers, grandparents, and friends. Like all newborns, she was the source of hopes and expectations for her family and friends. Most importantly, her parents wondered, often aloud, how she would add to the family constellation, how she would fit into and strengthen the family system. Prior to her arrival, her parents speculated about her possible relationship to her oldest brother, Nick, who happens to have autism and mental retardation. Will she understand? Will she still love him and accept him as her oldest brother? How will they interact? How will we explain Nick's disabilities in a clear, easy-to-understand manner? Her parents wondered how they would meet the challenges of caring for this new family member, as well as for their other children, one of whom requires more time, more patience, and more parental resources. Cate's parents wondered if they would find the help they needed from other family members, friends, and the professionals who worked with their son Nick.

In June, Michelle graduated from the eighth grade. Two weeks before the ceremony, alone in the car with her mother, Michelle asked, "Does Timmy have to come to the graduation?" All of her friends would be there with their families. Michelle felt that they would all be staring at Timmy, who is ten years old, does not speak, is not toilet trained, and has frequent and loud tantrums. "Why does he always have to come? Can't we get a baby-sitter?" Michelle's mom was a bit taken aback. They were a strong, close family—despite the challenges Timmy posed. After some initial debate, Michelle's parents found a baby-sitter. As they left for the graduation, Michelle said to her parents, "You know I love Timmy. He's my brother. It's just hard for me sometimes. Thanks for treating me special too!" Somehow Michelle had learned to talk openly and honestly with her parents. No doubt she learned this because her parents took the time to listen to her and recognize her unique needs and concerns.

For years, parents, brothers, and sisters have grappled with the task of raising and living with children with developmental disabilities. There is no single guidebook, no Dr. Spock-like reference, no family atlas to make the journey easier. Likewise, practitioners working with families in which one member has a disability have long recognized the need for a book that is written for brothers and sisters, but which would also help parents and professionals. What was needed was a book to help siblings sort out and deal with their many and mixed feelings of anger, joy, confusion, jealousy, fear, love, guilt, and pride. What was needed was a book that would explain disabilities in a factual, easy-to-understand manner. What was needed was a book that would present specific strategies to help brothers and sisters meet the unique and often intense challenges of living with a sibling with a disability.

Don Meyer and Pat Vadasy, professionals with substantial experience with and deep understanding of and sensitivity to the needs of siblings and families, recognized all these needs. Through their efforts, we now have a book written especially for brothers and sisters. We have a book that deals directly with sensitive topics in a matter-of-fact manner, drawing on the experiences of the many siblings with whom the authors have worked. Finally, we have a book written by individuals who are familiar with the literature and the scientific research, and who can present complex material in straightforward and clear language.

A few characteristics of this book need special attention. Throughout, the authors use many vignettes about and quotes from siblings. I especially enjoyed the brief story of Charlie, Mike, and Tony at the Special Olympics. It made me stop, think, and reconsider what siblings learn when they grow up with a brother or sister with disabilities.

The organization of the book reflects the notion that all siblings, no matter what disability their brother or sister has, share a number of unique concerns and needs. The first chapter, which is my favorite, deals with these real concerns and needs. "What do I tell my friends about my sister Monica?" "Why do I feel angry, sad, happy, embarrassed, and jealous?"

The authors not only discuss these concerns and needs, but also explain them in a fashion that enables siblings to understand that they are a normal part of growing up. This chapter provides ample suggestions to siblings on how to deal with friends and parents, as well as their own emotions, and on ways to interact with the child with disabilities.

The first chapter provides a strong foundation for the next chapters, which detail various disabilities. The authors provide clear, concise, and current information for siblings. These chapters will help dispel myths and misconceptions about particular disabilities, leading to a better understanding and acceptance of the disability.

The final chapters on educational services and the future bring universal sibling themes back into focus. Siblings, like their parents, need to understand human services and are often anxious about the future. Again, the emphasis here is on sharing information.

Although written especially for siblings, it would be a shame if this book were read only by brothers and sisters. It also has a clear message for parents and professionals. It should be read and reread by moms and dads, as well as by anyone attempting to help families. We will all learn to better help siblings after reading this book.

It seems to me that Don and Pat write so well because they recognize the importance of siblings in the life of children with disabilities. They understand the importance of siblings in the family system. Their comments and suggestions are pragmatic because they took the time to listen to siblings and understand their needs and concerns. Because they took the time, our job as parents and professionals will be much easier.

One final note, before you begin to read this book: Do not expect a heavy, "oh-woe-is-me" attitude. This book is exciting and unique because it is so positive, so up-beat. The book stresses the positive outcomes of living with a brother or sister with a disability, while recognizing the difficulties.

I expect that this book will have a significant, positive impact on the lives of families. *Living with a Brother or Sister with Special Needs* will serve as a standard for future works for and about siblings. I hope this book finds its way into local libraries and schools and into the hands of all sisters and brothers who are faced with the challenge of living with a sibling who has a developmental disability.

Thomas H. Powell
Dean, School of Education
Winthrop University
Rock Hill, South Carolina

A Note to Brothers and Sisters

We have a friend, Paul, who's twelve years old. Paul is like a lot of junior high students. He plays soccer and computer games with his friends. Sometimes they hang out together after school and listen to music and talk. But there's something Paul doesn't talk about with his friends: his sister Emily. Emily, who is six, is deaf and has mental retardation. Some days Paul would like to tell his friends how angry he is at Emily for getting into his room and destroying his things. Other days he'd like to tell them how proud he is of Emily when she learns something new—like how to make the sign for dog, or how to eat without making a huge mess. But Paul doesn't talk about Emily to his friends. They wouldn't really understand.

There are *thousands* of children like Paul who have brothers or sisters with special needs. But Paul is luckier than most of them. He has a place where he can go and talk about Emily with others who *do* understand. Every month or so, Paul attends a Sibshop, which is like a cool club just for brothers and sisters of kids with special needs. Paul likes Sibshops, because they are designed to be fun to attend. While they are definitely not like school, kids learn things during a Sibshop—like how computers help people with disabilities, or what it feels like when a physical therapist rolls you over a therapy ball.

Along with the "new games" and other activities, Paul and other kids have a chance to talk. They talk about the good and not-so-good parts of having a sib with special needs. Sometimes they offer each other advice. Sometimes they laugh, knowing that what has happened to them has happened to others, too. They talk about things that maybe they can't tell their parents or friends–like what you do when your sib loses it at a shopping mall. Or what you do about classmates who say mean things about people with special needs. Or how to tell your parents that you would like to spend some special time just with them.

Paul has made two friends at Sibshops–Rosa and Marty. While they don't live in the same neighborhood, they talk on the phone at least once a week and always look forward to seeing each other at Sibshops. Paul doesn't feel quite so lonely with his feelings anymore.

We wish there were Sibshops all over the country. Although there are more all the time, there still aren't enough. It would be great if sibs everywhere could talk to another sibling who understands. Brothers and sisters should know other kids who also might have some mixed feelings about their sibs with special needs. They should be able to get answers to their questions about disabilities and about the ways that people with disabilities are helped.

These are the reasons we wrote this book. It doesn't cover every disability, but we tried to write about the most common ones, and the questions sibs have most often asked us. We couldn't write about every feeling that a sib has, but we tried to write about the feelings that kids discuss at Sibshops. We think it helps to know that you aren't the only one who feels the way you do.

We wrote this book for *you*—the brothers and sisters of kids with special needs. Because you are a sib, you are the only one who can tell us if the book helps you. You can tell us if we have answered your questions about your sib's special needs, and if we have written about the feelings that *you've* had. To let us know how we have done, we have included some questions at the end of this book. Please help us by answering the questions after you have used this book. (If this is a library book, just photocopy the page or write the answers on a separate sheet.) Many of the changes we have made in this new edition are suggestions made by brothers and sisters. We want this to be the best book possible for sibs of kids with special needs.

One last thing: Because this book talks about lots of special needs, you don't have to read it cover-to-cover. Feel free to skip around. Use the table of contents and the index to find topics that interest you. However, be sure to read Chapter 1, "What It's Like to Have a Sibling with Special Needs." If your sib's behavior sometimes gets to you, you might want to read Chapter 3 for suggestions. Chapter 7 is about services for people with special needs, and Chapter 8 is about the future. You may want to check these out as well.

A Note to Parents and Other Grown-ups

"Why did it happen?"
"Will she have to wear those thick glasses all her life?"
"What does Down syndrome mean?"
"Why did one twin get it and not the other?"
"Will he learn to read and write?"
"Will she be able to take care of herself?"
"What happens when we all grow up?"

When we listen to brothers and sisters long enough, we learn that they have questions about their siblings' special needs. This shouldn't be surprising–after all, parents of children with special needs have many questions about the cause and treatment of a child's disability. Why shouldn't brothers and sisters?

We have written elsewhere (*Sibshops*, 1994) that brothers and sisters have a life-long need for information regarding their siblings' special needs. To oversimplify siblings' informational needs, young brothers and sisters need to know that they didn't cause and can't catch their sibling's disability. School-age children need information to understand their siblings' special needs and to satisfy their own curiosity. They also need information to explain the disability to classmates and friends who will surely ask, "What's the matter with your brother or sister?" Teenagers, who begin to think about life beyond mom and dad, need to know about the family's plan for the future. Adult siblings, who will likely play increasingly active roles in the lives of their brothers and sisters with special needs, need information about housing and work alternatives, regulations, and agencies serving adults with disabilities.

We proposed the first edition of *Living with a Brother or Sister with Special Needs* more than ten years ago because we could not find materials written specifically for young brothers and sisters. Since that time, there have been modest increases in the availability of written materials for young readers about disabilities. However, much remains to be done.

At the Sibshops we have run over the years, we have tried to provide siblings with information that they would find helpful. As useful as Sibshops may be, however, they still have their limitations. Because most Sibshops are for brothers and sisters of children with various disabilities, it is difficult to say very much about any one disability. Books, such as this one, have their advantages. A book can reach more siblings than we ever could individually. We can provide detailed information on more types of disabilities than we can at a workshop or Sibshop. We can offer siblings who still do not have a Sibshop in their community the solace that goes with knowing that there are other brothers and sisters who have ambivalent feelings about their sibs with special needs. Readers can use the information in a book whenever they feel like it, and go back to it again and again. And parents can read sections to children who are too young to read on their own.

In preparing this revised edition, we incorporated the suggestions that our young readers and others have made about the first edition. We sent chapters on disabilities, services, and legislation to authorities who provided us with helpful comments and up-to-date information. New sections were written on attention deficit hyperactive disorder, fetal alcohol syndrome, fragile X syndrome, traumatic brain injuries, ultrasound, speech therapists, Maternal Serum Alpha Fetoprotein, the Americans with Disabilities Act (ADA), and the Individuals with Disabilities Education Act (IDEA). Every sentence in the book has been analyzed (using readability software) and rewritten to assure that the information we present is accessible to as many young readers as possible.

Our friend Debra Lobato (1990) wrote that children's understanding of their siblings' special needs "will represent a unique blend of what they have been told, overheard, and conjured up on their very own" (p.21). We know this from our own experience. When we first met with siblings and asked them to tell us what caused their brother's or sister's disabilities, we found that they often had basic questions and misunderstandings. Here are some things the siblings wrote:

"I don't really know what caused it."
"I think it was mom's stomach."
"It was the amount of cromozomes."
"A piece of steel fell on mom's leg when she was pregnant."

"It was childbirth."
"It was too much excitement."
"The bag broke."

Siblings also shared with us problems they experienced as a result of having a brother or sister with a disability.

"Friends make fun of her."
"He bites me."
"She embarrasses me when she sucks on her hand in front of my friends."
"If kids make fun of her I tell them to stop or I'll sock them."
"Sometimes I cry without knowing why."
"When he screams it scares me."
"I get embarrassed when strangers stare and think she's dumb."
"It's hardest when people laugh and she doesn't know what she's doing wrong."
"Mom needs to spend a lot more time with him than with me."

Consistently, brothers and sisters have told us that they need and appreciate information:

My advice is that doctors and parents ought to give information to the brothers and sisters straight! Sometimes, instead of telling them the truth, parents and doctors tell siblings a lot of baloney. It is easier to handle when at least you have all the facts. (Maria, age 15, in Murray and Jampolsky 1982, p.43)

We have sought to provide young brothers and sisters with helpful information, offered in a straightforward manner. We hope you will read and share *Living with a Brother or Sister with Special Needs* and let us know how we did.

Acknowledgments

So many people helped as we prepared the second edition *of Living with a Brother or Sister with Special Needs* that we hardly know where to begin.

Preparation of this edition was supported, in part, by the Department of Education's Program 84-029K, Training Personnel for the Education of Individuals with Disabilities—Special Projects, Office of Special Education. We are most grateful for the support from the Department and from our project officer, Dr. Angele Thomas.

We consulted many specialists as we prepared this new edition to be sure that the information we present is as accurate and up-to-date as possible. We want to thank the following individuals for reading and suggesting changes and additions to the manuscript to assure that the book you are holding is useful to young readers: Kari Ciaciuch, Dr. Marcia Davidson, Erica Lewis Erickson, Amy Faherty, Debby Ingram, Dr. Joseph Jenkins, Gail Karp, Arlene Libby, Patricia Lott, Dr. Jeff McLaughlin, Mary Marin, Christine Polyzos, Dr. Ilene Schwartz, Cynthia Shurtleff, and Scott Truax.

Finally, we owe our largest debt of thanks to the many brothers and sisters who provided the encouragement and inspiration for this book. We have now met hundreds of young brothers and sisters across the United States–either at Sibshops or through the mail. The questions they have posed and the issues they have raised have shaped the content of this book. This book is their book. We hope they will let us know how we have done.

Living with a Brother or Sister with Special Needs

Chapter 1

What It's Like
to Have a Brother or Sister
with Special Needs

If you are reading this book, there's a good chance that you have a brother or sister who has a disability or special health problems. There is also a good chance that you have questions about your brother's or sister's special needs. You may have feelings that you think no one would understand, not even your best friend. Maybe you get embarrassed by your brother when he makes noises at church. Or perhaps you feel angry when a classmate says something mean about your sister who has a disability.

You probably have good feelings, too. Like being proud when you teach your brother how to do something all by himself. Or feeling relieved when a friend defends your sister from name-calling. Some of these feelings are hard to talk about, because who would understand?

Maybe you've thought that you are the only person who has had these feelings. But most brothers and sisters of children with special needs have these feelings sometimes. These feelings can help you grow and understand things about life that take other people a long time to learn.

In this book, we'll talk about experiences and feelings you may have had—the good ones *and* the not-so-good ones. We will also discuss some of the special qualities that siblings like you have—qualities that make you a special person.

Friends

Sometimes, friends need to be reminded that
a person with a disability is still a person.

Kevin was so angry he wanted to kick something—or, better yet, someone. As he and his friends finished their basketball practice, a group of wheelchair athletes came into the gym to play basketball. Before they left, Kevin and his teammates watched the athletes roll their wheelchairs on the court and begin to play. Just as they were leaving through the gym door, one of Kevin's teammates yelled—loud enough for everyone to hear, "Hire the handicapped! They're fun to watch!" Some of the other kids laughed. Kevin, whose brother has cerebral palsy, said nothing. All that night and the next day he had a knot in his stomach.

Chen wishes people would understand that he and his sister are two different people. Chen and his twin sister Helen go to the same school. He is in the sixth grade and Helen is in a class for children who have special learning problems. Although Helen tries, she has trouble reading anything harder than a book for second graders.

At recess or after school, Chen and his friends sometimes tease each other. That's usually okay, except when they call Chen a "retard" because his sister needs special help in school. He tries to ignore it because he knows that if he gets mad, his friends will tease him even more. Still, it hurts a lot.

Melissa hates to bring her girlfriends home. Kelly, her older sister, has a disability and doesn't have any friends in the neighborhood. So whenever Melissa brings friends home to play, Kelly barges in. She always wants Melissa's friends to play with her stupid little dolls. Most of Melissa's friends are polite to Kelly, although a few of them will look at each other and snicker when Kelly starts up. Then Melissa gets red in the face and sometimes wishes Kelly would take a long walk and not come back.

Friends are great to have and important to all of us. But for some brothers and sisters of children with special needs, friends can be a special problem. Here are some problems sibs may have with friends:

4

- Friends sometimes make fun of children who are different, maybe even your brother or sister.
- Friends may tease you. They may say that because your sibling has a disability, you must have one too.
- When your friends are around, things your sibling does may embarrass you.

People who tease and make fun of kids with special needs usually don't know any better. They probably feel awkward because they haven't been around people with disabilities very much. They might even feel nervous or afraid when they are around people with special needs. They don't know how to act. They might think that making someone else feel bad will make them feel better. People who tease usually are only looking at how the person with the disability is different on the outside. They don't know that on the inside, people with disabilities have feelings too. They haven't learned yet that all human beings have special qualities. And they don't realize how much their words can hurt—both the person with the disability and the people who care for him, like Kevin.

Most sibs say they wouldn't make friends with someone who makes fun of people with special needs. But there are times when your good friends may say something mean or thoughtless about someone with a disability. They may call the kids in special education "retards," or make fun of how they walk or talk. When friends do this, it can make you feel bad because you really like these friends but you love your sib too. What can you do?

First, don't join in with them just to be part of the crowd. This will only make you feel guilty later (see page 13). Let your friends know that making jokes about someone's disability—something that a person can't change—is not fair. Often when people see a person with a disability, all they see is the disability. They need to be reminded that behind the disability is a person. A good way to do this is to point out some of the person's qualities. If your friend laughs at the unusual way a child walks, you might say something like "Yeah, but have you ever seen him smile? He's got a great laugh and he's really a neat kid."

If your friends make fun of your special sib, let them know that it makes you feel uncomfortable, sad, or angry. You might try saying, "I feel bad when you make fun of my sister. She may have a disability, but she's my sister and I don't like it when you do that. It's not fair."

Also, if your friends tease you, like Chen's friends do, by saying that you must

What It's Like to Have a Brother or Sister with Special Needs   5

be retarded because your sib has learning problems, let them know how you feel. Let them know that you and your sibling are two different people. You could tell them, "I'm not my brother. Just because he has a disability doesn't mean I do. If he had his choice, he wouldn't be disabled either. It bothers me when you make fun of his problems. Please stop it, okay?"

Most friends will stop when you ask them. They may not realize that the teasing bothers you. That's why it's important to tell them. *How* you tell them is also important. You will be more successful if you talk to your friend privately—not in front of other kids. Tell your friend how you feel. Tell her in a way that makes it clear that you care about her friendship. Talking it over in private is much better than getting upset at your friend when you are in a group.

But what if friends keeps saying mean things after you have told them how their words and actions make you feel? The sibs we have talked to say that you might want to look for new friends! Good friends will listen to you and will not want to hurt your feelings.

Sibs often ask us what they should do when they want to invite a new friend or a date home. They may worry about what their friends will think of their brother or sister. One very good way to deal with this problem is to explain your sib's disability *before* your friend comes to your house. This makes it easier for both of you when your friend meets your special sib. Remember to tell your friend about your sib's good points. Here's how one sib told a friend about her sister: "Just so you won't be surprised, there is one thing you should know before you come over on Saturday. My sister Janet has cerebral palsy. She had some problems when she was born that hurt some parts of her brain. She uses a wheelchair and can't talk, but she can understand what people say to her. She has a great sense of humor and real pretty hair." A few words can go a long way to help you and your friend feel at ease. Anyway, chances are that you will notice your sibling's looks and behavior more than your friends will.

Finally, some sibs have problems with their brothers and sisters—special or not—hanging around when friends come over. Your sib may want to join in what you are doing, or may pester you or your friends for attention, like Kelly does to Melissa. If your sib bothers you to get attention, try ignoring her behavior. Read the section on "Behavior Problems" (page 56) for ideas about how to successfully ignore a sibling's behavior. If this doesn't work, consider going to your room or to a part of the house where your sib is not allowed to go. You may have to get your parents to help.

6

If you don't want your sib to hang around when your friends are visiting, let your sib and your parents know—in a calm way. This doesn't mean that you won't want to include your sib in activities at other times. But for the next hour or so, you would like to visit with your friends alone. If your sib has trouble understanding or accepting your explanation, try promising some special time together later. This may satisfy your sib so you can be alone with your friends. But be sure to keep your promise!

Though Bonita has a severe disability and can't see, she knows her brother loves her.

Unselfishness

Unselfish people give without expecting anything in return.

Even though she has a severe disability and can't see, Bonita's a lucky little girl. She has an older brother, Jerome, who's crazy about her. He puts her in her stroller and takes her out for walks and sometimes sings her songs, which make her smile and laugh. More than once, he's even changed her dirty diapers. Still, some of Jerome's friends wonder why he spends time helping a sister who can't see or walk or play games. One of his friends actually asked him why he did it. Jerome replied, "Because I know if I was disabled and Bonita wasn't, she'd do the same thing for me."

Unselfishness is caring about another person and not expecting to get something back from them. Many brothers and sisters of people with special needs—like Jerome—are unselfish. They do things for their sibs with special needs even though they know their brothers and sisters can't give back in the same way. Unselfish people care about other people, even those who aren't good-looking, popular, or smart. Someone once said that the best way to judge a person is to see how he treats someone who can't do anything for him or to him. An unselfish person sees what is good in each person, even if a person has a disability.

Anger

It's okay to get angry—even at a sib who has special needs.
But what is important is how you get rid of those angry feelings.

For over a week, Sarah had worked on a seven-page report for school on the history of her state. On Sunday night, after she finished the report, her brother Mike, who has mental retardation, decided to "color" her report with a purple crayon. Sarah caught him and got very angry. She screamed at Mike, "Don't ever touch my homework again!" Mike didn't understand why Sarah was yelling at him and he began to cry. That made Sarah feel bad. She wanted to teach Mike a lesson, because she had put a lot of work into her report. She was disappointed and discouraged when Mike wrecked it.

Anger is a strong feeling we have when someone mistreats or hurts us. It's what you feel when your sister punches you, or when your brother borrows your comic books without asking. Siblings often get mad at each other, even in families where no one has a disability. It's okay to get angry—even at a brother or sister who has special needs. After all, anger is part of life. It's also okay to get rid of those angry feelings that build up inside. But there are good and bad ways of releasing those feelings. It's better to release them so that the person understands why you are angry than to yell and make the person feel scared or hurt. What is important is how you get rid of those feelings.

When people express their anger, they sometimes say that they are "letting off steam." In many ways, anger is like the steam that operates a steam engine. A steam engine uses pressurized steam, as energy, to turn the engine. Anger, used correctly, can be a kind of "energy." It can let people know how you feel and why you are upset, so they can change the way they behave. But anger, like steam, can hurt people if not used correctly. Steam that is released from an engine can burn someone who gets too near to it. Anger can hurt someone if it is released all at once or in a thoughtless way. Most of us can remember a time when someone was extremely angry with us because of something we did. Their anger may have been so great that they were mean to us or frightened us.

Holding in anger doesn't help. A steam engine that never released its steam would eventually explode. But how do you let out anger so it helps instead of hurts?

How to Talk about Your Anger

One good way to talk about your anger is to use "I-statements." I-statements let others know how you feel and why you feel that way. An I-statement begins with the word "I" and goes on to describe how you feel and what makes you feel that way.

In our example, Sarah screamed at her brother, "Don't you ever touch my homework again!" If she had used an I-statement, Sarah might have said firmly, but without screaming:

"I am really angry that you scribbled on my report!"

("I" + how you feel + what makes you feel that way)

I-statements are very clear when used correctly. They are especially valuable when you want to let your special sib (who may need clear instructions) know exactly why you are angry. The better your sib understands why you are angry, the easier it will be for him or her to behave differently.

I-statements are also a safe way to blow off steam. They don't say anything

Sarah screamed at her brother, "Don't you ever touch my homework again!"

bad about the person, they only talk about what the person did. There is no room in an I-statement to call someone a "bad boy," a "jerk," or an "idiot."

Below are examples of angry statements that aren't clear and probably would hurt more than help. Underneath each angry statement is an I-statement that would be a better way of expressing your anger.

Angry statement: "Cut it out, pea-brain."
I-statement: "I don't like to be tickled when I'm trying to watch TV."

Angry statement: "Stay out of my closet, you slob!"
I-statement: "I really get upset when my clothes are borrowed without my permission!"

10

Angry statement: "Turn that down! Now!"
I-statement: "It hurts my ears when the radio is turned up so loud!"

Angry statement: "Get out of here and don't come back!"
I-statement: "I don't like to be bothered when I'm trying to visit with my friends."

Angry statement: "I don't want to ever see you near my tapes again!"
I-statement: (Try this one on your own!)

Remember the formula for an I-statement:
"I" + how you feel + what makes you feel that way.

When you need to let someone know you are angry, think about what that person did to make you angry. Then, put together the I-statement that will let the other person know most clearly why you are angry.

Accepting Differences

Accepting differences is something that siblings
of children with special needs learn when they are still growing up.

When Robin and her friends returned to school last year, there were a lot of changes. Not only were there two kids with disabilities in her class, but there were three new Vietnamese students. Nobody knew how to act around the new Vietnamese students. Hardly anyone talked to them, because they couldn't speak English very well. One day at recess, Robin's friend Anne said, "I don't know what's happening to our school. First we have the weirdoes from the special ed classes, and now we have these foreign kids. Look at the clothes they wear! School's just not the same."

Robin was surprised at what Anne had said. Robin's oldest brother Bill has Down syndrome. When he was younger, he had to take a bus to a school that was far away from everyone else's. Robin liked the idea of all kinds of kids going

What It's Like to Have a Brother or Sister with Special Needs 11

to school together now. Also, she thought the Vietnamese kids made school more interesting. There were already white, African American, and Native American kids at school, so why not Vietnamese kids? In a funny way, it made the school feel like a little United Nations.

Some people won't have anything to do with people who are different. Some people won't accept a person who is a different color, race, or religion, or who differs from them in other ways. They are intolerant. This means that they can't accept other people's differences. You often find that the intolerant person doesn't know much about those people. People are often intolerant of others because they have never been around someone of a different race or religion. They don't really understand how much they are like someone whose race is different, and how little they differ.

If you have a sib with special needs you have probably noticed that some people leave your sib out of activities and conversations—just because she has special needs. You may have classmates—like Anne—who won't play with the kids with special needs. If these classmates took the time to get to know kids with disabilities, they might find that they have a lot in common. They would learn that their special classmates like the same computer games, music, or sports that they like. They would probably be surprised to discover how much a person with a disability *can* do. They might even learn that their classmates with disabilities are better at some things than they are!

"Tolerance" means accepting people and ideas that are different. For some people, it can take a long time to learn tolerance. Tolerance is something that siblings of special children like Robin learn when they are still growing up. Your experiences with your special sib help you understand that people who have differences or disabilities still have a lot to offer. They can even make good friends, if you take the time to get to know them. People like Anne—who don't take the time to get to know people who are different from her—may never find that out.

Sometimes, even brothers and sisters have a hard time accepting their sibling's disability. It may bother them so much that their sib is different that they dislike or avoid their sibling. If you ever feel like this, you should talk to your parents or to a trusted relative or friend. You could also ask your teacher or parents if you could talk to a counselor to help you understand your feelings.

Guilt

Guilt is what we feel when we blame ourselves
for doing something we think is wrong.

"Supper's almost ready," Joel's mother announced as he was watching TV. "Will you go down the block and tell Benjamin it's time to come home?" Humph, thought Joel as he left the house, Why do I always have to go get that kid in the middle of my favorite TV show?

"Benjamin!" Joel yelled impatiently as he walked down the block. Joel thought about how his brother, who has mental retardation, was always screwing up his life. "Benjamin! It's time for supper!" He continued yelling for Benjamin all the way down the block until he reached the corner. Benjamin was playing kickball with kids younger than he was. "Benjamin, you idiot!" Joel roared. "Didn't you hear me calling you? Boy, are you stupid!"

Benjamin looked down at the ground and his lower lip began to tremble. He was about to cry. Walking home, both boys were quiet. Benjamin was upset that his brother had yelled at him. Joel felt rotten because he had called his little brother a stupid idiot. Benjamin didn't need to be reminded that he was slow. He knew that.

"Dear diary," wrote Vanessa, "I have a terrible secret that I have never shared with anyone. Before my brother Christopher was born, I was the youngest in our family. You might say I got a lot of attention from my folks and my brothers and sisters. When I was four, my mom told me we were going to have a new baby in the family. I wasn't too happy about that news. Just before Christopher was born, I had what I guess you'd call a 'temper tantrum' and my mom got real upset at me. Two days later my mom had Christopher. I remember that he couldn't come home from the hospital right away because something was wrong. Chris is now eight years old. He acts very strange, can't read, and the few words he can say usually don't make sense. Dear diary, my terrible secret is that I think Chris's problems are all my fault!"

Guilt is a terrible feeling. We feel guilty when we blame ourselves for doing something we think is wrong. Sometimes guilt is useful, and sometimes it's useless. It helps to know what kind of guilt you are feeling.

What It's Like to Have a Brother or Sister with Special Needs 13

Joel felt rotten because he had called his little brother a stupid idiot. Benjamin didn't need to be reminded that he was slow. He knew that.

Useful Guilt

Useful guilt is feeling bad about a situation that you helped cause. It is the feeling you may have after you say something mean about a classmate. Or when you hit your sib for drawing in your books. Or pretend that you don't know your sib when you are out shopping.

Although useful guilt is painful—as Joel knows—it can help you. It can help you see how you can change for the better. It can help you act in ways that are kinder in order to avoid the guilty feelings you suffer later.

If you feel guilty and think about how you acted (by listening to your feelings), you may decide:

• Saying mean things about your classmate was not very kind. You may decide he didn't deserve those mean words and that you wouldn't like someone talking about you that way. You probably won't do it again.

14

- It was unfair to hit your sister for drawing in your book. It was okay to get angry at her (see "Anger," page 8), but hitting didn't help at all. She cried, you felt bad, and she *still* didn't learn not to draw in your books.
- You don't need to pretend you don't know your brother with special needs when you go out shopping. After thinking about it, you may decide that you are proud of your brother's accomplishments. Even though he has a disability, you want to let others know that you are proud of him. Of course, if he is having behavior problems at the store, ignoring him may be the best way to stop the problem. For some tips on ignoring, see the section on "Behavior Problems" on page 56.

Useless Guilt

Useless guilt is feeling bad about a situation, or the way things are, even though you didn't make them that way. You may feel this kind of guilt when you win first prize in a poster contest. You feel good that you won, but you feel bad because your friend also worked very hard and wanted to win. You may feel guilty when you think about your good health or grades and then think about all your sibling's problems. You may wonder why you were lucky and he wasn't.

Or you might blame yourself for your sister's disability, like Vanessa did. You might think that something you said, did, or thought somehow caused your sib to have special needs.

Feeling guilty about these things is useless because, if you think about it, they are not your fault. You did not cause the situation that makes you feel guilty.

- Both you and your friend did your best on the poster contest, but you won. In a spelling or a baking contest she might win, even though both of you would try very hard. Good friends wouldn't want you to feel guilty for winning. They might be disappointed they lost, but they would also be happy for you.
- You may be able to do many more things than your sib can, but this is not a good reason to feel guilty. Remember, just as you want him to do the best he possibly can, he wants you to do the best you possibly can.
- There may be many reasons why your special sib has a disability. Some of those reasons may still be a mystery to the doctors and your parents. But none

of those reasons are your fault. Upsetting your mother when she was pregnant or playing rough with your baby sister did not cause her to become disabled. Her disability was probably caused by something that no one could control or prevent.

When you feel guilty, ask yourself these questions: Is the guilt useful (do you feel bad because you helped cause the situation, like Joel did)? Or is it useless (do you feel bad, like Vanessa, even though you didn't cause the situation)? If it's useful guilt, it can help you act in a way that is better for others and yourself. It can teach you to be caring. If it's useless guilt, get rid of it. This kind of guilt won't help you or anyone else. Don't let it waste your time or take your attention from more important things. If you just can't help feeling bad, talk about your feelings with your parents, teacher, school counselor, or a friend.

Jealousy

Sometimes you probably feel like saying,
"Hey, you have other kids in this family too!"

I know this sounds crazy, Emma thought to herself, but sometimes I wish *I* had cerebral palsy! Lately Emma has been feeling jealous of her sister Amy, who has cerebral palsy. It seems to Emma that Amy gets all the attention. Emma's soccer games never seem as important to her mother as meetings at Amy's school or at the Cerebral Palsy Center. If Emma brings home a paper with a B grade, her mother says, "Well, you'll have to try harder next time." But she makes a big fuss about anything Amy brings home, no matter how sloppy it is. When Amy was the state cerebral palsy poster child, Emma stayed with her aunt while Amy got to meet the governor at the TV station. It's just not fair, Emma thought.

If you have a brother or sister with special needs, chances are that sometimes you feel neglected. You might feel ignored by your parents. It may seem that they don't notice you unless you do something wrong or get into trouble. They may spend so much of their time on your special sib that you feel left out, as though you're not very important. Sometimes you probably feel like saying,

16

I know this sounds crazy, Emma thought to herself, but sometimes I wish I had cerebral palsy!

"Hey, you have other kids in this family too!" You want to let your parents know your sib isn't the only person in the family. Like Emma, you might sometimes wish that you had a disability, just so you would get as much attention as your sibling.

Parents usually have to spend more time with a child with special needs than with the other kids in the family. The special sib often needs medical care or help to do things that you can do for yourself. Some special sibs need lots and lots of attention. Others need extra help only in certain areas. But just because your brother or sister needs extra attention doesn't mean that you don't need some attention too. You still need to spend some time with your parents, talking about your problems and doing the things that your friends do with their parents. You

What It's Like to Have a Brother or Sister with Special Needs 17

need to spend an afternoon at the movies together, or go out for ice cream, or go to the swimming pool. When parents have a special child, they sometimes forget that all of their children need some of their time and attention.

If, like Emma, you feel that your parents are ignoring you, try telling them just how you feel. If it's hard for you to tell your parents how you feel, try practicing with a good friend. Some people like to practice in front of a mirror. Tell them you understand that your special sib needs a lot of their time. But remind them that there are times when you need attention too. Tell them that you would like to spend some special time together, and do things you both enjoy. When you're done, let them know how good it feels to know that they are there for you when you really need them.

Overinvolvement

A family member who is overinvolved puts too much time and energy into caring for the child with special needs.

To most adults, Marty probably sounds like a perfect son and brother. Every day, he comes straight home after school. Marty takes care of his brother Paul, who has spina bifida, so his mom can go shopping and run errands. Marty plays games with Paul, fixes him snacks, takes him for walks, helps him with his school-work, and sometimes even gives Paul a bath. But while Marty is doing all these things, there are a lot of things he isn't doing. Marty isn't in the school play, he isn't playing football, he isn't hanging out with his friends, he isn't learning to play the guitar, he isn't reading books. Marty, you might say, is *overinvolved* with his brother Paul.

To be overinvolved means to be too close to something or someone. An over-involved family member is someone like Marty who spends all his free time with his brother. At first glance, that may not sound like a problem. After all, you and your parents want to do everything you possibly can to help your sib with special needs. A family member who is overinvolved, however, puts too much time and energy into caring for the child with special needs. The over-involved person neglects his own life.

Overinvolvement can hurt all family members. The overinvolved person may not have any energy or time left for other people and other interests. Overinvolvement also leads to "burnout"—running out of energy and new ideas. Burnout can even hurt the child with special needs. When the overinvolved family member runs out of energy, the child with special needs may no longer get the special care and attention she needs.

How can you prevent being overinvolved? Family members can do this by reminding themselves that *everyone* in the family has needs, not just the child with the disability. For example, you need to make friends, practice basketball or soccer, and spend time with your parents. Family members need to spend time with each other and pay attention to each other, even when one member has a disability. Because of the child's disability, everyone may have to give up *some* time and attention. But no one should give up so much that he or she stops growing as a person.

Understanding

It takes time to understand how hard it is for someone with a disability to do things that most people don't even think about. But you understand.

Margaret was sitting with her classmates at a school baseball game. Everyone was watching the member on the opposite team who was getting ready to bat. He walked to home plate with an uneven limp. It looked as though he either had cerebral palsy or had been in an accident. At his side was another boy who would run the bases for him. Margaret admired his courage for getting up there and showing everyone what he could do. It reminded her of her brother Tom, who has cystic fibrosis. Even though it is often difficult, Tom always tries to do his best at whatever he does. Secretly, Margaret hoped that the batter would knock the ball out of the park and score a home run, even though he was from another school.

There is an old American Indian saying, "Do not judge a person until you have walked twenty miles in his moccasins." This saying explains a lot about understanding—sharing another person's emotions and knowing how that person feels. Siblings of people with special needs, like Margaret, are often understanding of people who are different. Because they have grown up with someone with special needs, these brothers and sisters appreciate the everyday challenges and difficulties that people with disabilities experience.

Embarrassment

Sometimes you just want to pretend you don't know your special sib.

Only an hour ago Michelle couldn't wait to go shopping for school clothes at the mall. Then her mother told her that her sister Jenny, who has multiple disabilities, would be coming too. Now she dreaded the idea.

This is just what I need, thought Michelle to herself. She had just started junior high. What would happen if the kids from her new school saw her at the mall with Jenny? And that awful wheelchair? And her drooling? And the way she bites her hand? It wasn't that Michelle didn't love Jenny, but she hadn't forgotten other times when Jenny had embarrassed her. Like the noises she once made during the quiet part of the band concert that Michelle had played in. Or the puddle Jenny made last Easter when she peed in her wheelchair, right outside of church. . . .

Does your special sib drool? Make loud noises? Act or look unusual? If so, you may feel embarrassed when you are out in public together, or when friends come over to your house. You may be so embarrassed by your sib that you don't invite your friends home (see pages 4-7), or you avoid going out with your sib in public.

For most of us, like Michelle, being like everyone else is pretty important. A special sib can make that hard sometimes. Your sib may do things that seem strange and different. If this happens, try to remember that people's differences make the world interesting. Some people have different religions. Some have different skin colors. But they still have many things in common. Your brother may look different. He may not walk the same way other children do, but chances are you have many things in common. Are there things that you and your special sib both like, such as TV shows, ice cream flavors, or computer games? Are there things that you and your sib both dislike, such as vegetables, chores, or homework? In the end, the ways in which people are the same are more important than how they differ.

If your sibling has embarrassing behavior problems, sometimes these problems can be helped by special programs (see "Behavior Problems," page 56). You will probably want to ask your parents to help you work on your sib's embarrassing behavior problem. Let your parents know that there are certain things that your brother does that embarrass you. Ask them if the whole family could work on those things.

Other times, you may be embarrassed by things you cannot change, such as your sister's drooling, braces, crutches, or the way she looks. The stares and looks you get just walking with her in a shopping mall may make you feel uncomfortable. In fact, at certain times, they may make you very unhappy, like Michelle. When this happens, you might need a little space. That's okay. Even though you sometimes need space doesn't mean you don't love your sister or that you aren't proud of her (see the section on "Pride," below). It doesn't mean that you won't want to spend time with her in public later on. It just means that for right now you need to put a little space—a little distance—between you and your sister. That's okay.

Pride

*You're proud of your sib's special qualities
even if other people only see his special needs.*

"C'mon Tony! C'mon Tony!" shouted Charlie and Mike from the stands at the Special Olympics. On the field is their brother Tony, who has Down syndrome. Tony is short and round, but he was biting his lip and swinging his arms furiously as he raced toward the finish line.

"Yay! All right! Wa-hooie!" screamed Charlie and Mike as Tony crossed the finish line in second place. As soon as Tony stopped, he pushed up his glasses on his nose. He looked at his brothers in the stands, smiled, and flashed a "V for victory" sign with his fingers.

On their way down to the field to congratulate him, Mike thought about what a neat kid Tony is. Sure, he could be a royal pain sometimes, but look what he did today! He couldn't remember ever being so proud of his little brother.

Mike couldn't ever remember being so proud of his little brother.

People who don't know someone who has a disability often don't realize that people with special needs also have special qualities, just like anyone else. You often don't find out about these special qualities until you get to know a person. But, because you know your sister so well, you know her special qualities— maybe better than anyone else in the world. These qualities make you proud. You feel proud of how good your sib is at some things, like swimming, or running, or playing wheelchair basketball, or saying things that make you laugh. And you also feel proud because you know how hard it is for your sib to learn to do some of these things.

Other people may only see what your brother or sister *can't* do. They see, for example, that your sister isn't as smart as her classmates, that she can't see, or can't walk without crutches. And that's all they see. But if they took the time to get to know her, they would understand why you and your family often feel like bragging.

For example, John's brother Dave has a learning disability. Dave has a very hard time spelling, reading, and writing. He often stays inside and works on his homework when his friends are outside playing. Even though it took him longer than his classmates, Dave is learning to read, and he can now read some easy books all by himself. John knows how hard it was for Dave to learn to read. John feels very proud of Dave because he tries so hard.

Or there is Susan's sister Jennifer, who has mental retardation. At first, some of Susan's friends thought it was funny when Susan bragged about Jennifer. They knew that Jennifer was in a special class. They thought, what could be good about having a sister who has all those problems? Jennifer is a lot slower than other kids her age, and she can't do things like multiply, count money, or even play video games. She looks different, too. But now that they know Jennifer, they understand why Susan is so proud of her. Susan is proud of the way Jennifer has learned to take care of her room, fix a simple meal, and swim. Susan knows that these things are harder for Jennifer than for other girls her age. Knowing this makes her even prouder when Jennifer learns something new.

Gary has cerebral palsy. People often stare at him and feel sorry for him because he can't walk or talk. But his sister Sara knows that Gary can do some wonderful things, like operate the special computer that is attached to his wheelchair. Gary takes his computer to school and to the store. He can order a milkshake with it or do his homework on it. He can even play games on it. Sara knows that Gary has a great sense of humor and he often writes jokes on his computer. People who don't know Gary may feel sorry for him. But Sara has watched Gary learn to communicate, and she can think of many reasons to feel very proud of him.

Brothers and sisters are often proud of their siblings who have special needs. They know that what someone *can* do is more important than what they can't do.

Loss

Some things just won't be possible for your sib with special needs. Knowing that can make you feel sad.

Tonight, sitting on her bed, Sally was feeling sad. Yesterday her brother Gene had left for college in another part of the state. That left Sally at home on the farm with her parents and her sister, Danielle. Danielle is a year older than Sally, although you'd never know it. Danielle has some chromosome problem that Sally has never really understood.

Sally thought to herself: Even though Gene is older and we fight sometimes, at least we can talk. That's impossible with Danielle. Why can't I be like my friend Jan? Jan and her sister do things together, share a room and tell each other about school, friends, and boys they like.

As she stared out her bedroom window Sally thought: I wish I had a sister I could at least talk to.

Did you ever want a dog or CD player for your birthday and get a sweater instead? At the time, you were probably disappointed. But after a while, you might have decided a sweater was okay. It did keep you warm, and it looked great with jeans. Still, you really wanted something else. In a way, you feel a sense of "loss," because you lost the thing you really wanted—the dog or the CD player.

Loss is a special sadness and disappointment that people feel when something they wanted so much just isn't possible.

Siblings like Sally feel a sense of loss when they have a brother or sister who has a disability. If your special sib is a baby, you may not be able to play with him the way you could if he didn't have special needs. If your special sib is older than you, you may miss having an older brother or sister who can help you and show you how to do things. Instead, *you* may have to teach your older sibling how to do things. You may also feel sad that your sibling cannot do all the things you can do, such as ride a bike or go to a dance. Like Sally, you may miss having a brother or sister who can share secrets with you or give you advice. Sometimes you feel cheated because you miss out on things your friends enjoy with their brothers and sisters.

Your parents also felt a sense of loss when they first learned that your sib had special needs. They had to give up some of the dreams they had for their child. Many things they wanted so much for all their children will not be possible for your special sib. They may have to accept that your sib will not go to college, or play basketball like your dad did, or get married and have a family.

It takes a long time for everyone in the family to get used to these losses. Sometimes it helps to tell someone—maybe your parents, an aunt or uncle, a good friend, or a trusted teacher—how you feel. Even if the other person can't change

24

things, just sharing your feelings with someone you are close to can make you feel less sad.

Maturity

Many adults who grew up with siblings with special needs say they learned things that have made them wiser and stronger.

One evening Kerri was in her room getting ready to go to the movies with her friends. Her parents were also going out. It was their anniversary, and last week Kerri's mom had bought a new dress to wear to dinner.

The telephone rang and Kerri heard her mom answering it. Mrs. Randle, the baby-sitter, was calling to say that her daughter had just come down with the flu. She wouldn't be able to baby-sit with Lee that evening.

Kerri bit her lip. Lee, her brother, has epilepsy, like one of Mrs. Randle's children. Kerri's parents never worried when Mrs. Randle baby-sat for Lee. Ever since Kerri had started junior high, her parents had tried to get a baby-sitter for Lee on weekends so Kerri could go out with her friends.

Kerri heard her dad say he would have to call the restaurant and cancel their reservation for dinner. She came out of her room and said, "You and mom get your coats on or you'll be late. I'll stay and watch TV with Lee."

Kerri's mom gave her a big hug. The look of pride her dad gave her made her feel very grown up.

Today in Patrick's family-life education class everyone was going to get a chance to feed a real baby. This year all the sophomores were taking the class. They were learning things like how to change diapers and how to hold babies the right way. Most of the girls did okay, but some of the boys got pretty nervous. Patrick's friend Sam looked scared when the teacher brought one of the babies over to their group. Patrick offered to be first and fed the baby some applesauce.

"How'd you get so good at that?" Sam asked. Patrick just shrugged. His sister Lizzie has cerebral palsy. All the kids in his family had helped to feed and dress her and take her to the bathroom since she was a baby. Patrick didn't even think much about it. Everyone in the family had just learned to help Lizzie until she could do some of those things for herself.

What It's Like to Have a Brother or Sister with Special Needs 25

After years of helping out with his sister Lizzie, feeding a baby was no big deal for
Patrick.

Your life as a sibling of a child with special needs is different in some ways from
the lives of your friends. You may have certain responsibilities, like Patrick does,
for baby-sitting, feeding, or teaching your special sib. Your parents may trust
you to do things that take extra patience, dependability, and time. You have
probably already done things that are hard to do—like answering a stranger's
questions about your brother or sister. Or maybe, like Kerri, you gave up something you wanted to do to take care of your sib. These experiences all add up
to something called maturity, which means being grown up.

   Many adults who grew up with a brother or sister with special needs say that
their siblings helped them learn many things. What they learned made them
stronger and wiser adults. They feel they are more understanding and patient
as a result. These are qualities that make a person mature.

Your responsibilities and the way you have learned to think of others' needs have made you mature, like Kerri and Patrick. But if you have too many responsibilities, you can't develop other qualities that are also important.

Sometimes, parents of a child who has special needs forget that their other children are not fully grown up, no matter how mature they may be. If you feel that you spend *too* much time taking care of your special sibling, talk to your parents. Let them know that you do not have time to do other things you would like to do. It's important that no one in the family have too many responsibilities caring for the family member with special needs. When everyone pitches in it helps everyone in the family. All family members need time for themselves so they can do things they enjoy.

Worry

If you have a sibling with a disability, you have different things to worry about than most of your friends.

Last month, Allen's parents sat the whole family down and told them the news: Tyler, Allen's new little brother, has Down syndrome. "He'll be just like us in almost every way," his mother told them, "except it will take him longer to learn."

This year Allen is having a terrible time in math. He almost flunked his last two tests. Today, when he had a hard time again on his math test, Allen wondered: Maybe I have Down syndrome, too?

Jenna went with her family to an Arc family picnic last summer. At the picnic, Jenna saw many adults with disabilities. It made her think about her brother, who has a lot of problems. Will he live to grow up and go to school and get married, she wondered. Or will his problems get so bad that he dies?

At her cousin's wedding, Pam started thinking about her own future. Like her cousin, she wants to get married and have children someday. Still, she wondered: If I have children, will they be deaf like my sister?

If you have a sibling with a disability, you have different things to worry about than most of your friends. You might wonder about things that could happen to you or your brother or sister. In one of the examples above, Allen is worried that he might have Down syndrome like his brother. Since family members are alike in many ways, with the same color hair and eyes, and similar features, you may worry that you have what your sib has. Kids at school may even say things about your special sib that hurt your feelings and make you wonder if you have problems too. It would help if Allen talked to his parents, teacher, or doctor about Down syndrome. He would find out that disabilities *aren't* something you catch, like a cold, or something that all family members share. By talking to one of these people he could also find out what caused his brother's disability. Often, worries can be cleared up just by talking to someone!

Jenna thought about her little brother: Will he grow up or will his disability get so bad he dies?

28

Like Jenna, you may worry about *what will happen to your brother or sister* when you and your sib grow up. No one can ever tell for sure what a child will be like when he or she grows up, especially someone with a disability. But we do know enough about many disabilities to know what happens to most children when they become adults. If you can talk to your parents, ask them questions about the things that worry you. If it is hard to talk to your parents, you could also ask your teacher, family doctor, school counselor, or aunt or uncle. You might even try someone from your church or temple or even a favorite librarian.

If you are curious about *who will take care of* your sibling when he or she grows up, ask your parents. You deserve an answer! Sometimes parents don't realize that the other kids in the family are worried about the future (see page 111). Your parents may have plans for your sib's future that they have not explained to you. Once you understand what plans your parents have, you will feel better. You will have a clearer idea of what the future holds for your brother or sister, as well as yourself.

Like Pam, most siblings at one time or another worry whether their own children will have special needs. As we explain in Chapter 8, "The Future," this depends on what kind of disability your sibling has. Does your sibling have a *hereditary* disability? By hereditary we mean, did they "inherit" this condition from a parent who had it or was "carrying" it? If your brother or sister's disability is hereditary, there *might* be a chance that your child could have the disability. If your sib's disability is hereditary, or if your parents are not sure what caused it, your family should contact a genetics clinic. Your parents may already have this information to share with you. A genetics counselor or your family doctor can help you understand what your chances are of having a child with your sib's disability. Genetics clinics are found in most medical schools and large hospitals.

However, if your sibling's disability resulted from an accident during or after birth, your chance of having a healthy baby is as good as anyone's.

Worries are like mushrooms. They grow best in dark places. Nothing gets rid of worries faster than to get them in the open. Moms and dads and other grown-ups like teachers and doctors can help. They can give you the facts that will explain away many of your worries.

It can also help to talk to other siblings. Like you, they know all about living with a brother or sister with special needs. In some cities there are special

What It's Like to Have a Brother or Sister with Special Needs 29

programs just for brothers and sisters. At one such program, called Sibshop, brothers and sisters mostly have fun, but they also talk about what is on their minds. The Arc (see page 38) or Parent-to-Parent program in your community may be able to tell you if there is a Sibshop in your area. We talk about other ways to contact siblings in the next section.

Loneliness

*It's easy to feel alone when there is no one to understand
the special joys and challenges that you face daily.*

When kids in his class start talking about their brothers or sisters, Jason gets very quiet. He doesn't say much about his special sister, Erin. What would he say? Who would understand?

Suppose one girl bragged about how her brother won a prize at the Science Fair. What would Jason say? How proud he is that Erin, who is ten, can finally go to the bathroom by herself? Jason is proud of Erin all right, but who would understand?

If a classmate complained about her sister always getting into her things, what could Jason say? That his father had to put a lock on his door to keep Erin out, because Erin doesn't know any better? Once she completely wrecked a model spaceship he had almost finished. No, his friends wouldn't understand.

Just once, Jason thought, I'd like to meet another kid who has a sister like Erin.

To feel lonely is to feel sad and different from your friends. Children, like Jason, who have special siblings can sometimes feel alone. They might feel that no one understands the special joys and challenges they face daily. They may not feel that they can talk about their special sib with their friends. Most friends don't know how it feels to have a sister who has special needs.

Parents with children who have disabilities can also feel lonely or isolated if they don't know other parents who share some of the same special concerns. Luckily, in many cities and towns there are groups where parents can meet other parents of children with special needs. At these groups they talk about their worries and feelings. Talking about things with someone who knows what you're going through can help you feel less lonely.

For some sibs, just talking to their parents can help them feel less lonely. After all, parents know many of the challenges that children with disabilities can cause their sibs. In some families, though, no one talks about the child's special needs. For them, the disability is just too hard to discuss.

When no one talks about the disability, it can make brothers and sisters feel lonely. They can't discuss it with anyone who really knows how they feel. It can also cause confusion, because sibs grow up without knowing much about their own brother's or sister's disability.

Everyone who has a person with special needs in the family should have someone to talk to who understands their feelings. If your parents can't or won't talk to you, try one of your other sibs, a favorite aunt, a grandparent, a teacher, or a friend. Another good way to feel less alone is to meet other kids who have sibs with special needs.

It can be great to meet and talk with other sisters and brothers of children with special needs. They can understand your good feelings and not-so-good feelings in a way that other friends can't. Just talking with them can make you feel better. In some parts of the country, groups for siblings of children with special needs are starting to pop up. (In some places they are called Sibshops.) At these groups, sibs meet other sibs, talk, make new friends, and usually have a good time.

Unfortunately, some parts of the country don't have groups for sibs yet. If there isn't a sib group in your area, there are other ways to meet brothers and sisters of kids with special needs. Ask your parents if your sib's school is planning a picnic or party for the children's families. Ask if they could have something special, just for the brothers and sisters. If not, tell them you would like to meet some other sibs. You can also ask your teacher or guidance counselor if they know any other sibs of special children in your school.

Books and other materials can help a sib feel less alone. In this book we talk about the feelings, joys, worries, and questions that sibs often have. There are many other books about siblings of children with specific handicaps, like blindness or cerebral palsy. Look at the list of kids' books about special needs starting on page 121. Many are stories about a boy or girl who has a sibling with special needs. It can help to curl up with one of these books and read about someone who has gone through some of the same things you are going through.

What It's Like to Have a Brother or Sister with Special Needs 31

In the following chapters we move from talking about feelings to facts. We present information to answer questions that many siblings have about their brother's or sister's disability. We also write about services and treatments available to help children with special needs.

If you don't want to read the whole book, that's okay with us. Just check the table of contents to look for parts that are interesting to you. Be sure to read the last chapter, though. It's all about you and your sib's future!

Chapter 2

Mental Retardation

Mental retardation is a term used to talk about children who are much slower than other children their own age. Children with mental retardation take longer to learn most things—both in school and at home. Some children who have mental retardation can learn to do many of the things you can do. They will learn how to talk, ride a bike, or take a bus. It will just take them longer. Other children who have mental retardation will not be able to learn all these things.

If your brother has mental retardation, you probably know how it affects him. Compared to other kids, it probably took him longer to learn how to walk and talk. In fact, he may *still* not know how to walk and talk. It may take him a long time to learn other things—like how to count money at the store or dress himself. If he is in school, he may be in a special class. In this class, his teacher can take time to teach such things as how to read, count, tell time, and spell.

What Causes Mental Retardation?

Sometimes, something that happens *before* a child's birth causes mental retardation. Some disabilities, such as Down syndrome (page 75) or spina bifida (page 70) start before a child is born. They can also cause mental retardation. A baby can be hurt before birth in other ways. If a pregnant woman has a serious injury or disease or is exposed to certain drugs, it can hurt the baby she is carrying. The injury to the baby sometimes causes mental retardation.

There are other causes of mental retardation. Being born too early, problems at the time of birth (see "Anoxia," page 79), certain diseases, poor environments, and accidents that cause brain damage (page 82) can also cause mental retardation.

Mental Retardation Affects Some People More Than Others

Mental retardation affects some people a lot, and others much less. People will have different needs, depending on how serious their retardation is. Psychologists, teachers, and others who work with people with mental retardation try to learn about their strengths and needs. Knowing their strengths and needs helps professionals determine how much and what kind of help they will need in school. It also helps them know how much help people with mental retardation will need to hold a job and live away from home.

People Needing Intermittent Support

Some people with mental retardation will need only *intermittent* help or support. *Intermittent support means that the person will need help now and then.* People who need intermittent support learn more slowly than other people their age. They may look, run, and walk like anyone else. However, they may have more trouble learning to talk, using their hands, following directions, and remembering things.

Some people who need intermittent support may not seem different or slow, except in school. At school, they will have trouble learning in most subjects. Most are able to learn some reading, writing, and math skills. When they grow up, they have a good chance of holding a job and living on their own. Some may get married and have children.

People Needing Limited or Extensive Support

Other people with mental retardation will need *limited* support. *Limited support means that they may need help over a short period of time.* Limited support helps them through changes in their lives. These changes can be going to a new school or starting a new job or moving into a place of their own.

Still others will need *extensive* support. *Extensive support means that they may need help every day to do things like get dressed for school or cook or clean their house.*

Sometimes people need extensive support in one area of their life. But in other areas they only need limited support. For instance, Marshall needs extensive support managing his money and paying his bills. However, he needed only limited support learning his job at the recycling center. How much support a person needs all depends on how much that person has learned to do on his or her own.

People who need limited or extensive support learn things more slowly than people who only need intermittent support. As children, they are often very slow to walk and talk. They can have trouble remembering things. They may be clumsy. They have learning problems at school and at home. They will need a lot more help learning to take care of themselves than other children do.

People who need limited or extensive support may look or act differently than other people. Even so, they may work in a real job in their community when they grow up. They will need extra help from a job coach to learn the job. They may also live outside their parents' home. They might live in a home with other adults who have mental retardation, or they may live in a home or apartment with someone who can help them when they need it. We know some people who live in apartments with limited help. They receive help from a counselor who helps them learn living skills, such as cooking, shopping, doing laundry, and managing their money.

We know some people with mental retardation who have boyfriends and girl-friends. With support and classes on relationships and decision-making, some choose to get married. Because raising children is such a serious responsibility, people who need limited or extensive support usually do not have children. Those who do decide to have children need help from others to take care of them.

People Needing Pervasive Support

Finally, some people with mental retardation will need *pervasive* support. *People who need pervasive support will need help from someone else to do almost everything, even brushing their teeth or getting dressed.* These people may never learn how to talk, and sometimes they do not learn how to walk. At school, these children learn how to take care of themselves by learning how to eat, drink, and move around. Many of these children also have other disabilities, such as epilepsy, cerebral palsy, problems seeing or hearing, or serious health problems.

These children will need a lot of help for their many needs all of their lives. When they grow up, they may live in a group home or in the community. During the day they may attend special programs. At these programs they learn new skills and enjoy the company of other people. They may learn enough to work in a sheltered workshop or in supported employment (see page 114).

Developmental Disability

"Developmental disability" is an "umbrella" term that includes many problems that affect how a child grows and learns. People with mental retardation are said to have a developmental disability. There are other people who do not have mental retardation but still have a developmental disability.

The U.S. government has an official definition of developmental disability. This definition helps the government decide who can get special help, such as medical care and special education. According to the government, a developmental disability must be a severe condition that is a result of mental or physical disability, or both.

> Antonio's Down syndrome causes him to have a mental disability. Mark has cerebral palsy. Although he has a physical disability, Mark is very smart. Both Antonio and Mark have "developmental disabilities."

To be a developmental disability, the condition must also be "chronic" meaning that the problem won't go away.

Rochelle uses a wheelchair because she has cerebral palsy, a condition that does not go away. Amy uses a wheelchair because she broke both legs skiing; she'll walk as soon as her bones heal. Even though Rochelle and Amy both use a wheelchair, only Rochelle has a developmental disability.

Finally, the disability must occur before the person's twenty-second birthday.

Julia, who has a head injury from an automobile accident when she was four, has a developmental disability. Thomas, who also has a head injury from an automobile accident he was in when he was thirty-one, does not have a developmental disability.

How many people have mental retardation?

For every 4,000 people in the world, approximately 100 have mental retardation.

(1)   (2)   (3)

(1) Intermittent need for support, (2) limited or extensive need for support, (3) pervasive need for support

For every 100 people with mental retardation approximately 85 will have intermittent need for support. Twelve of the 100 will have limited or extensive need for support. Only 3 of the 100 will have pervasive need for support. In the United States, approximately 7,200,000 (7.2 million) people have mental retardation.

Common types of developmental disabilities are mental retardation, cerebral palsy, deafness, autism, and blindness.

An excellent source of information about mental retardation is your local chapter of The Arc (a national association on mental retardation). Your phone book lists this organization under "The Arc" or under the old name of "Association for Retarded Citizens" or "ARC." You can also write or call the national office to get the address of your nearest Arc chapter:

The Arc
500 East Border Street, Suite 300
Arlington, Texas 76010
Phone: 1-800-433-5255

Chapter 3

Disabilities That Affect How People See, Hear, Speak, Learn, and Behave

Disabilities can change the way we experience the world. In Chapter 2, we explained how mental retardation can limit a child's understanding and the way that child experiences the world. For instance, mental retardation can make it hard for a person to understand the many rules and regulations about driving. Because of this limitation, driving a car is an experience this person may not ever have.

Disabilities that affect children's senses will also affect their experience of the world. We use our senses—especially our sight, hearing, and touch—to take in information. When our sight or hearing is impaired, we miss out on the information we normally get from these senses. We use speech to describe our experiences and convey information. When our speech is impaired, it can interfere with our ability to tell others about our experiences.

In this section we talk about disabilities that affect vision, hearing, and speech. We also talk about learning disabilities and problems that affect how children behave. Finally, we'll suggest some ways of helping a sib who is having a behavior problem—even if that sib doesn't have a disability!

Vision Problems

They say that my brother Michael is "legally blind" but he can see some things. Some people don't think Michael can see at all! What does the word "blind" mean, anyway?

I have a brother who is blind. Sometimes his blindness makes me mad. Because he is blind, we have to do things like keep all the doors closed. A door that is a little bit open can really hurt my brother when he bumps into it. We also always have to put things away in their place because my brother can't look around for things like I can. While being careful all the time is no fun, my brother can be a lot of fun. We play games (his are in Braille). We go for walks (he uses his cane). We talk about everything (he can't see, but boy can he talk!). When I make him mad, he finds me and we wrestle until we both start to laugh (he's a good wrestler!). Sometimes I worry that he will have a bad life because he is blind, but I know that he can work, have a family, and enjoy life—just like me.

Have you ever heard someone say "I have 20/20 vision!"? "20/20" means that a person can read the figures on a Snellen eye chart at a distance of twenty feet. Someone who is "legally blind" has vision that is "20/200" or worse, *even when they are wearing glasses or contacts*. This means that people who are legally blind can still read things. But they can only read at twenty feet things that people with 20/20 vision can read at two hundred feet! Most people who are legally blind can see enough to perform some tasks.

Some babies are born blind or with a partial loss of vision. When they are *born* with vision problems, they have a "congenital" vision problem. These vision problems can be caused by a disease a mom had during her pregnancy, such as German measles. Sometimes, children "inherit" vision problems from their parents. This can happen when the parents also have a vision loss, or if parents "carry" a condition that causes the loss. Babies that are born with certain syndromes may have vision problems as well.

Some children lose their sight *after* birth. In the United States, the most common cause of blindness is cataracts. Cataracts are a clouding of the lens of the eye. They sometimes occur in children who are born with German measles or have Down syndrome. An injury to the eye can also cause cataracts. Cataracts

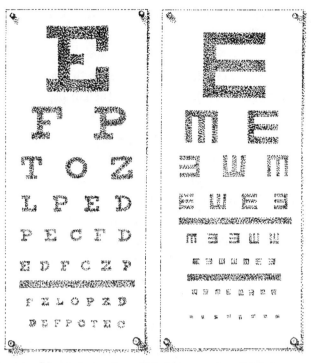

A Snellen eye chart, on the left, and an "E" chart on the right. A person reads down the Snellen chart as far as he or she can. A person who can read the bottom line from 20 feet has 20/20 vision. The "E" chart is used with children and people who cannot read.

can be helped when an eye surgeon removes the clouded lens and replaces it with a substitute lens.

Babies who are born too early (premature infants) sometimes develop retinopathy (ret-i-nop'-a-thee) of prematurity, which can cause permanent blindness. This happens when they receive too much oxygen. They need the oxygen to live, but too much oxygen damages the blood vessels in an infant's retina.

Another cause of blindness is glaucoma (glaw-coe'-ma). When a person has glaucoma, fluid in the eye builds up and the pressure damages the inside of the eye. A person may be born with glaucoma or may develop it during child-hood. Glaucoma is treated with eye drops or surgery.

I have to wear glasses, even though my vision is not too bad.
What causes vision problems like mine?

Mild vision problems often result from changes in the normal shape of the eyeball. These changes prevent light rays from focusing properly on the retina. When the eyeball is too long, the person is said to be "nearsighted" or have myopia (my-ope'-ee-ya). This means the person can't clearly see things that are far away. When the eyeball is too short, the person is said to be "farsighted" or have hyperopia (hi-pur-ope'-ee-ya). This means that the person has trouble seeing things that are close. These problems can be corrected with glasses or contact lenses. People can be both nearsighted *and* farsighted. These people often wear special glasses called bifocals.

My brother's eyes look in different directions. What makes this happen?

Other vision problems are caused when the muscles that move the eye do not work together. Strabismus (stra-biz'-muss) is the inability to focus both eyes on the same object. Our eyes send two separate pictures to the brain, not just one. When a person can't focus both eyes on the same object, the brain ignores the images from the weaker eye. This can result in another condition—amblyopia (am-blee-ope'-ee-ya), which is a loss of vision in the eye that grows weak from not being used. Amblyopia can be treated when the child is young by putting a patch over the strong eye. This forces the weak eye to get stronger. Special exercises can also help to strengthen the weak eye.

Blindness is not very common in children. Only one out of every 2,500 children is blind. About half of the children who are blind are born that way. About 40 percent lose their sight before they are one year old. One-fourth of blind children have no sight at all. The rest can detect light or see well enough to read very large letters.

It is fairly easy to identify an infant who is totally blind. Normally, babies use their sense of sight to follow objects and reach for toys. Infants who are totally blind will not do these things. It is more difficult to tell when an infant has other vision problems. If doctors are worried that a baby has a vision problem, they can perform special tests. During these tests, doctors watch how the baby moves her eyes, how she reaches for toys, or how well she recognizes pictures.

Vision problems can slow a child's development. It will take a child who is blind longer to learn to reach for objects, sit up, crawl, walk, and even talk. Children who are blind may also have some unusual behaviors. They may rock back and forth, bang their heads, or even put their fingers in their eyes. They do these "self-stimulatory" behaviors because they feel good in some way.

Most of us learn a lot about our world just by looking. Because of this, children who are blind and children with vision problems need extra help to learn. For example, babies who are blind can't see that what they do affects things and people around them. They don't know that when they smile, their family members smile back at them. They learn about emotions other ways, such as through touch, tone of voice, and people's descriptions of what is happening.

They may need help to learn to play with toys and use objects. They need to touch things and hear descriptions to learn about them, such as how objects fit together. To learn to talk, just like sighted children, they will need to hear names of the objects they touch and may need a description of how the object is used.

Hearing Problems

Hearing is one of the senses—just like vision, taste, touch, and smell. Like other senses, hearing helps us learn about our world. Hearing also helps us learn to speak. By listening to others we learn that certain patterns of sounds—words—refer to certain objects, actions, and emotions. When we were babies, hearing helped us learn that we can make the same sounds and patterns of sounds that others make. First we babbled, and then we learned to talk and communicate through speech.

There are three parts to an ear: the outer, middle, and inner ear. When you hear, sound is captured in the outer ear and travels down the ear canal. This makes your eardrum move. Three tiny bones in your middle ear—called the ossicles—respond to the eardrum's movements. The ossicles send a message to the cochlea in the inner ear. The cochlea sends the message along to the hearing nerve, which passes the message to the brain stem. Finally, the brain stem passes the message to the brain.

Hearing loss can be caused by problems in the outer, middle, or inner ear. Many things can cause a hearing loss. Here are some of them.

Disabilities That Affect How People See, Hear, and Speak   **43**

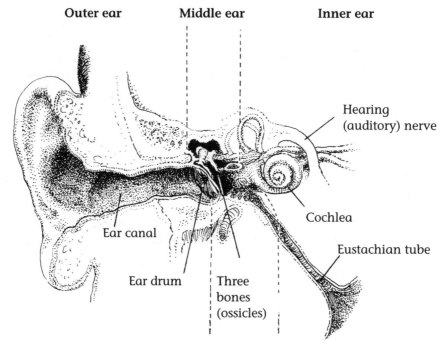

Outer ear   **Middle ear**   **Inner ear**

Hearing (auditory) nerve

Cochlea

Eustachian tube

Ear canal

Ear drum

Three bones (ossicles)

Hearing losses can be caused by problems in the outer, middle, or inner ear.

Outer Ear Problems

Sometimes, a child is born with an ear canal that is not normally developed. When this happens, an ear doctor (an otolaryngologist) may surgically create an ear canal when the child is seven to nine years old. Or, if the inner ear is normal, the child may wear a special bone-conduction hearing aid that sends sounds directly to the inner ear.

Middle Ear Problems

Kids frequently get middle ear infections, which can be treated with antibiotics. However, if the infections occur too often, the doctor may put small tubes in the eardrums. The tubes drain fluid and let air into the middle ear, helping to protect the child's health and hearing.

Sometimes, the three little bones in the middle ear do not develop normally or become damaged from too many ear infections. In some cases, this can be corrected with surgery. If surgery can't correct the problem, a hearing aid may be needed.

Inner Ear Problems

The inner ear's cochlea is shaped like a snail shell and contains special "hair cells." Damage to these hair cells can lead to hearing loss. There are many ways that a person's hair cells can become damaged:

- If a woman is infected by a virus such as rubella, herpes, or cytomegalovirus (CMV) during the first three months of pregnancy, the virus can damage the hair cells in the ears of the baby she is carrying.
- A child can inherit a hearing loss from her parents. With some inherited problems, the inner ear does not develop during pregnancy. With other inherited problems, changes occur in the cochlea after the child is born, leading to a hearing loss.
- Meningitis is an infection that attacks the membrane around the brain and spinal cord. It can sometimes spread to the cochlea and damage the hair cells.
- Listening to loud sounds for long periods of time can damage the cochlea's hair cells. (Remember to wear ear plugs if you are going to be exposed to loud sounds, and keep the volume down on your walkman!)

The hearing nerve, also located in the inner ear, can be damaged by a severe injury. Because the hearing nerve connects the cochlea to the brain stem, this damage can also result in hearing loss.

Degrees of Hearing Loss

There are different degrees of hearing loss. People with a *mild hearing loss* can hear most, but not all, speech sounds and some environmental sounds. People with a *moderate hearing loss* can hear a few speech sounds and loud environmental sounds. People with a *severe hearing loss* can't hear any regular speech sounds and only louder environmental sounds. People with a *profound hearing loss* can hear only the very loudest environmental sounds.

Hearing Aids

Hearing aids can help people who have hearing losses in their outer or middle ears that can't be helped by surgery. They can also help people with hearing losses in their inner ears—if they have some hearing left. In most hearing aids, a tiny microphone picks up speech and environmental sounds. The hearing aid amplifies the sounds, and the amplified sounds are sent out through a speaker into the person's ear canal. The amplified sound makes the eardrum move . . . and you know the rest.

Cochlear Implants

Cochlear implants are new devices that can help some people who have profound hearing losses and can't use regular hearing aids. A part of the implant is surgically attached to the cochlea and stimulates the auditory nerve. Here's a brief idea of how they work:

Sounds are picked up by a tiny *microphone* that the child wears near his ear. The sounds are sent through a thin wire to a box that the child wears on his belt or in a fanny pack. The box contains a *speech processor*, which picks out speech sounds. The processor then sends the speech sounds through a wire up to a *transmitter*. The transmitter sits behind the ear and is held in place by a magnet. The transmitter sends a signal through the skin to a *receiver* that has been surgically inserted in the temporal bone, which is located just behind the ear. The receiver sends the message to the *cochlear implant*, which stimulates the auditory nerve. The receiver sends the message through a special plastic-coated wire, which stimulates nerve fibers that join to become the auditory nerve. The brain interprets this stimulation to the auditory nerve as speech.

The sounds heard by a person using a cochlear implant are different from the sounds we hear. Because of this, children with a cochlear implant need to practice listening with an audiologist. They will also need to practice talking with a speech therapist.

Sign Language

People who can't hear some or all speech sounds—even when wearing hearing aids—may use sign language. Sign language helps people communicate with their hands. Hand shapes and movements can stand for letters, words, or ideas. Here are the hand-signs for the letters in the English alphabet:

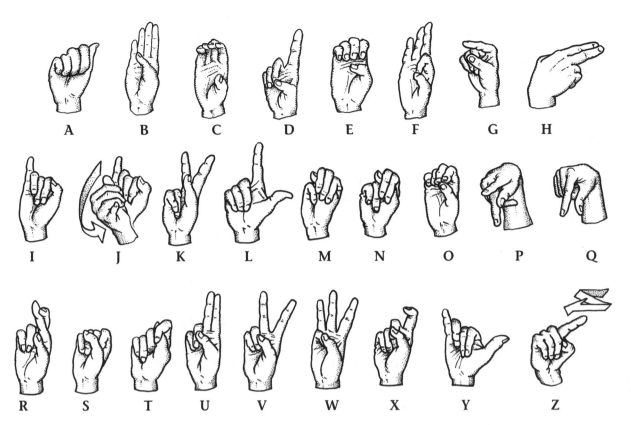

The hand signs for the letters in the English alphabet. Can you spell your name using hand signs?

How You Can Help Someone Who Has a Hearing Impairment

If you have a sibling or a friend with a hearing impairment, here are some ways you can help:

- It can be difficult for a person with a hearing impairment to hear when there are background noises. Moving out of a crowded room and turning off radios and TVs can help your sibling understand what you have to say.
- Make sure you have your sibling's attention before speaking. Make sure he has a full view of your face.
- If you stand too far away from your sibling, she might not be able to hear you. The closer you are, the better the chances are that your sib will understand what you say.

Disabilities That Affect How People See, Hear, and Speak   47

- Try to make sure that light is on your face. This will make it easier for your sibling to read your lips.
- Try not to speak too quickly. And never shout!
- Facial expressions and hand gestures can make what you say easier to understand.

Speech and Language Problems

Aren't speech and language problems the same thing?

People often use the words "speech" and "language" as if they mean the same thing, but they really are two different things. As a friend of ours puts it, "Speech is *how* you talk, and language is *what* you say!" Speech is making words with your mouth, lips, teeth, tongue, vocal cords, and lungs. Speech is only one part of language. "Language" includes many types of communication, like speaking, reading, writing, facial expressions, body language, and other ways of sharing thoughts and feelings. A child may have speech problems or language problems, or he may have both.

Speech Problems

What causes some people to sound so funny when they talk?

A speech problem makes it difficult for a child to talk and be understood. One common speech problem is stuttering. People who stutter may make sounds longer ("Thhhat's my dog"); or they may repeat sounds ("Wh-wh-where is my mom?"), syllables ("I'm go-going to-to-tomorrow"), or whole words ("Can can can Mike come to to play?"). People who stutter don't stutter on every word, and many can use their voice in ways so they sometimes don't stutter. For instance, Mel Tillis, the country-western singer, has a stuttering problem that does not affect his singing. Stuttering may be mild or severe. Although the cause of stuttering is not known, speech therapy for stuttering can be very helpful.

Kids with articulation (are-tick-yoo-lay'-shun) problems can be hard to understand. They often sound different from other children who are the same age

48

and speak the same language. A child whose mouth or throat has an unusual shape may have articulation problems. The unusual shape can make it hard for the child to form words. For instance, a person with a cleft lip and palate may be hard to understand because of the shape of his palate and lip.

When people have problems controlling the muscles that produce speech they often have articulation problems. For instance, people with cerebral palsy (which affects the ability to control muscles, see page 87) often have difficulty saying words clearly. Some children have nervous systems that are immature (or "too young") for their age. This can make it difficult for them to speak so others understand them.

No matter how hard she tries, you can't understand a word my sister says.

Sometimes, disabilities will prevent a person from ever talking clearly. When this happens, they may use a different type of communication, such as ASL (American Sign Language), the language of people who are deaf. Other people use a board with letters, pictures, or special symbols that help them tell others what they want.

Computers have helped people with disabilities. Special switches and keyboards allow them to type their thoughts and wants. Speech synthesizers can even "speak" the words they type to others. Some people with disabilities will use these boards and computers to visit with their friends and families. They'll also use them to let others know what they want to eat and when they need to go to the bathroom.

Some people with disabilities will also use their computers for school and work. We know one young woman with cerebral palsy who cannot use a keyboard. She controls her computer with a special head rest attached to her wheelchair. Using Morse code (a system of "dots" and "dashes" first used in telegraphs) she moves her head to complete her schoolwork. This system has helped her move from a special education class to regular education to where she is now—graduate school!

Language Problems

Why can't my brother understand me?

A child with a language problem has trouble communicating with other people. Children who have trouble understanding what other people say have a problem with their *receptive language.* They may not understand anything that is said to them, or they may understand single words only. Children with a receptive language problem may have trouble following directions. To help kids with receptive language problems, speech therapists (who work with kids and adults who have speech problems) suggest these ideas:

- Keep your talk simple so they can understand what you say. Instead of saying: "Remember last summer? It was just after we got out of school. We took that long, long trip in the van and camped along the way? And we saw Rachel, and she had that dog?" You could say: "Remember when we went to visit Rachel?"
- Don't ask them to do too many things at the same time. If you say "Angie, go put on your coat, get your doll and your knapsack, and meet me at the front door," she will probably get confused and may not do anything. A better way would be to do it one step at time: "Angie, put on your coat." Then, after her coat is on, give her the next step.

My sister can say words—they just don't make much sense.

Children who have trouble expressing their ideas to other people have problems with their *expressive language.* This can make it difficult to get along with others. To help sibs with expressive language problems, speech therapists suggest these ideas:

- Give them a lot of time to talk and get their idea across.
- Restate what they say, but say it in the right way. If your sib points to the door and says "Out!" you can say, "I want to go *out*side!"

Can people have expressive and receptive language problems?

People must be able to hear before they can talk. Because of this, children with receptive language problems (problems understanding what they hear) often also have expressive problems (problems expressing their ideas). For example, Shannon is a girl with an expressive problem. She only knows how to say a few words. She doesn't know the words for some things that other kids her age know. She doesn't know the "rules of grammar" that other children her age use. So, when Shannon wants a toy, she might say "Me want." She doesn't know the word for doll, and she doesn't know the rules to say "I want" instead of "Me want."

Many kids with language and speech problems don't have any other special needs. But children with certain disabilities often have problems with their speech or language. As we have mentioned, people with cerebral palsy, cleft palate and lip, and developmental disabilities may have speech problems. Children with Down syndrome may have articulation problems because they have poor muscle control. Children with hearing losses, mental retardation, emotional disturbance, traumatic brain injuries (TBI), or attention deficit hyperactivity disorder (ADHD) may have receptive language problems because they can't process what they hear.

Learning Disabilities

My little sister Rachel has a learning disability and needs special help in school.
Some kids call her retarded, because she goes to a special class. I know she's
not retarded, because she's really smart in a lot of ways.
What exactly is a learning disability?

Some children have special problems learning. These children may find it hard to listen, talk, think, read, write, or do math. Usually, kids with learning disabilities have trouble in the areas of reading, spelling and writing. Sometimes, learning disabilities make it hard for kids to learn math.

A learning disability is different from mental retardation (see page 33). A person with mental retardation is slower than others in all mental activities. A person with a learning disability usually does well with many thinking skills, but has real problems in some areas. For instance, Kaelin does well in reading, but he does poorly in other areas, such as math. People with learning disabilities can be as smart as anyone else. Some are even geniuses!

Most of us have problems with some things, like dribbling a basketball, ice skating, or singing on key. These weaknesses are not considered learning disabilities, because they do not usually affect how well we do in school. A learning disability makes it hard for a child to do well in school. Kristina, a girl who has a learning disability, has trouble paying attention to letters, remembering words, and putting sentences together. She has a tough time keeping up with her classmates.

Learning disabilities can also affect the way the child behaves in *and* out of school. Some children with learning disabilities are very active. They have a hard time paying attention, they get restless, and they may not do what they are told to do. Other kids with learning disabilities are slow and disorganized. They may start out to do one thing, forget what they were doing, and begin to do something else. Many children with learning disabilities behave just like their classmates outside of school.

A learning disability can affect everyone in the family. For instance Tashina is very active and sleeps poorly. In the morning, her parents are often tired and grouchy from being up at night with her. Tashina's sister Anita hates it when her parents are grouchy at breakfast! On the other hand, Kellin is very slow. He is never dressed on time to go to school, or is often late for dinner. Kellin's brothers really get angry waiting for him all the time, and they yell at him. Then Kellin's parents yell at his brothers for yelling at him, and soon *everyone* is mad.

Kids with learning disabilities can have trouble making friends and getting along with others. If they are clumsy, other children may not want to play games with them. They may sometimes forget the rules. Or they may embarrass their family and friends by saying the wrong thing at the wrong time, or making a scene in public.

What can family members do when a child has a learning disability?

All family members can help the child with learning disabilities get along better. Family members can help the child get organized and remember what to do. If your brother is always late for school, someone can lay out his clothes and schoolbag the night before. If he cannot remember things, give him very simple directions. For example, when Aaron's mom asked him to go to the store to buy milk and bread, he came home with just the bread. Aaron forgot what

A person with a learning disability may do well in some areas, but have a hard time in others.

he was supposed to bring home. After that, his mom always sent Aaron with a list to help him remember. Although you can't do everything for your brother, there are ways to help him do things for himself.

What causes learning disabilities?

No one knows exactly what causes learning disabilities. Children with learning disabilities often come from families with a history of learning problems. Learning disabilities are more common in boys than in girls. Teachers have many ways of helping students with learning disabilities learn to read, do math, and become more independent.

What happens to kids with learning disabilities when they grow up?

Some children with learning disabilities work very hard to complete academic programs in high school and go on to college. Some students need help with

Disabilities That Affect How People See, Hear, and Speak   53

their courses even in college. Some adults with learning disabilities continue to have difficulty reading, making change, or telling time. Other people with learning disabilities go to schools that teach trades or job skills. Or they may enter fields where they do not need to use difficult reading or math skills.

Attention Deficit Hyperactivity Disorder

Adrian, my brother, is a really wild kid. He has trouble at school all the time. My parents say he has ADHD. My best friend has a sister who has ADHD too, but she's not wild like Adrian. What is ADHD?

ADHD stands for attention deficit hyperactivity disorder. Many people also call it ADD, or attention deficit disorder, or even ADD/ADHD.

Children with ADHD can have problems with:

- *Inattention.* Inattention means that a person has a really hard time concentrating on one thing. Max is a boy with ADHD who has problems with attention. Max seems to pay attention to lots of things, all at the same time. When he is supposed to be paying attention to his teacher, Max is also paying the same amount of attention to other things, like the game being played outside the classroom window, the hiss of the classroom radiator, and his hungry tummy. Because he has trouble concentrating on just one thing, Max makes careless mistakes in his schoolwork. He has a hard time following instructions and organizing his schoolwork. Max often loses things.

- *Hyperactivity.* Tamara's parents say that she is hyperactive. Rachel, Tamara's sister, says "If you saw Tamara, you'd know why. She never walks when she can run. She climbs everything. She can't sit still, even to watch TV! I call her the 'human tornado.'"

- *Impulsivity.* In the middle of class, did you ever want to do something that you're not supposed to do? Like throw an eraser at your friend across the room, or make loud sounds when your teacher isn't looking? As tempting as it might be to do these things, most of us don't do these things after thinking about the consequences. People who have problems controlling their impulses often act *before* they think. They might run out into the street without looking, or wander outside the neighborhood without thinking about the

54

dangers of doing so. Gia's brother Tino is very impulsive. "He does whatever pops into his head—without thinking." Gia says, "He also says whatever pops into his head without worrying about other people's feelings. It is pretty embarrassing when my friends come over. He won't leave us alone and tries to tease me by saying that I like all these boys in my class."

Some people with ADHD may be *only* inattentive, *only* hyperactive, or *only* impulsive. Eric for instance, has no problem sitting still; however he does have serious problems paying attention. This makes it hard for him to do his schoolwork. *Most people with ADHD will have a combination of inattention, hyperactivity, and impulsivity.*

Sometimes I have problems paying attention, sitting still, and controlling my impulses. Do I have ADHD?

Probably not. People who have ADHD don't *sometimes* have problems with attention, hyperactivity or impulsivity. They *almost always* have these problems.

What causes ADHD?

Scientists think that ADHD is caused by a problem with chemicals in a person's body that help the brain regulate (or control) behavior. Even though there are still many questions about the cause of ADHD, scientists think it is a medical problem. It is *not* caused by parents or teachers!

How are people with ADHD helped?

Many people with ADHD will need special programs to help them learn and behave. Often, special medicines can help a person with ADHD. Kids with ADHD can have a hard time getting along with others. This can make them angry or feel bad about themselves. Counseling can often help. Because ADHD can be hard for *everyone* to live with, sometimes whole families get counseling!

Here are some books for kids about ADHD:

* *Learning to Slow Down and Pay Attention*, by Kathleen Nadeau and Ellen Dixon (ages 6-14)

- *Putting on the Brakes*, by Patricia Quinn and Judith Stern (ages 8-12)
- *Shelley the Hyperactive Turtle*, by Deborah Moss (ages 3-7)
- *I'm Somebody, Too,* by Jeanne Gehret (for brothers and sisters of kids with ADHD age 9 and up)

You and your parents may wish to get more information on ADHD from these two great resources:

- *Attention-Deficit/Hyperactivity Disorder: NICHCY Briefing Paper,* by Mary Fowler. Available at no cost from: NICHCY (National Information Center for Children and Youth with Disabilities), PO Box 1492, Washington, DC 20013; phone: 1-800-695-0285.

- CH.A.D.D. (Children and Adults with Attention Deficit Disorders), 499 NW 70th Avenue, Suite 109, Plantation, Florida 33317; phone: 305-587-3700.

Behavior Problems

My brother always bugs me when I'm trying to watch TV or mess around with my friends. How can I make him stop?

How many times have you heard your parents or teachers say "Behave yourself!" or "Quit misbehaving!" Learning how to behave, or act correctly, is part of growing up. Although it's sometimes hard to learn how to behave, most of us do learn eventually.

Some children have an extremely hard time learning how to behave. They may have special behavior problems that make life very difficult for them—and for the people around them. Below we suggest some ways of helping with a sib's behavior problem, regardless of his or her disability.

Behavior modification is one way of changing the way a person acts. A behavior is something a person does that we can see with our eyes. It is an action. For example, "sharing a toy" is an action, and so is "pulling hair." But "being nice" is *not* an action. Neither is "being mean."

"To modify" means to change. Behavior modification is a way of rewarding the actions we like and discouraging those we don't like.

Sometimes behavior modification is used at home and at school with children who have special needs. The term "behavior modification" usually refers to a carefully written plan for rewarding or changing behavior. But, in fact, our behavior is "modified" all the time!

Here are two examples of how rewards can change behavior: Let's say you learned how to juggle. Then, your teacher asked you to juggle at a school assembly. You juggled, you told jokes, you were great! You even received a standing ovation. All of a sudden, you are a *very* popular person. Do you think you would want to juggle in front of a group again? No question! Your behavior—juggling in front of an audience—was rewarded!

Here's another example: Your mom makes monster chocolate chip cookies for dessert. After dinner you hug her and tell her they were, without a doubt, the best cookies you've ever eaten. The next week, your mom makes cookies again. What does she bake this time? Monster chocolate chip cookies again! When you hugged her and told her they were the best cookies you've ever eaten, you "rewarded" her. By rewarding her you encouraged her to behave (make monster chocolate chip cookies) that way again.

In the two examples, the actions—juggling and baking cookies—were "positively reinforced." You can use positive reinforcement to help you get your brother or sister to behave in better ways.

Positive Reinforcement

When you reward behavior that you want to happen more often, you are using positive reinforcement. We get positively reinforced in many ways. Reinforcement can be:

- a hug from your parents for cleaning your room,
- a high-five from a friend for a good score on a video game,
- a smile from a pretty girl for helping her with schoolwork,
- or money from the next-door neighbor for mowing her grass.

We all have different ways we like to be reinforced or rewarded. Your sibling with special needs may have special reinforcers. He might like applause or praise when he does something you want him to do, such as putting on his socks or going to the bathroom by himself.

There is an important thing to remember, though. Positive reinforcement must not only make a person happy, it *must also increase the chances that the person will act that way again in the future*. Let's say that you would like your sister to help you clean the room you share. You tell her that if she puts her toys and clothes away, you will spend twenty minutes of "special time" with her. Your plan is to use "special time" as a "positive reinforcer" for putting toys and clothes away. But if your sister still refuses to help you clean your room, spending "special time" with you is *not* a good reinforcer—even though you know she loves spending time with you! You might have to try another reinforcer, like letting her play with one of your favorite things when your friends go home. A good reinforcer makes the person want to do a certain action more in the future.

You can use different things, like hugs or kind words, as reinforcers to increase good behavior. But what do you do about behavior you *don't* want? Ignoring it may help a lot.

Ignoring

One day, in class, Michael tried to get his best friend Janeel to talk to him. But instead of responding, Janeel did not look at Michael or talk to him! If you were Michael, what would you do? You might try again a few times, but after a while you'd probably quit trying to talk to Janeel. Ignoring can be a powerful way to stop behavior we don't want. Michael's behavior—talking—was stopped because Janeel ignored him.

When someone ignores you, you probably stop doing what you are doing or you try something else. Remember the juggling example described earlier? This time imagine a different scene. You juggle at your school assembly. Instead of watching, everyone reads books or talks to someone else. If this happened to you, would you want to juggle in front of the school again? Probably not!

Here is an example of how one sister used ignoring to stop her brother from doing something she didn't like:

> Amy's brother Stephen screamed and cried when he did not get his way. Tired of hearing him scream, Amy and other family members usually gave him what he wanted. Although they did not know it, they rewarded Stephen's screaming and crying.

Mr. Marshall, Stephen's teacher, suggested a plan to help Stephen with his tantrums. Mr. Marshall suggested that everyone in the family try to ignore Stephen when he has a temper tantrum. He said that if everyone ignored Stephen's outbursts, chances are he would soon stop. Amy and her family found that it was hard to ignore Stephen's tantrums! At first, Stephen screamed even more, but after a while he screamed less and less. He did not get rewarded with attention for having a temper tantrum. Amy and her family ignored the tantrum, but not Stephen. When he didn't tantrum, Stephen was included in the family's activities.

Here's an important thing to know about ignoring: When you first ignore a behavior you don't like, the unwanted behavior will probably increase for a

It used to be that when Stephen cried, his parents and sister would give him whatever he wanted. Now they ignore his screaming. As a result, he screams less and less. His screaming is not rewarded with attention.

Disabilities That Affect How People See, Hear, and Speak   59

while before it decreases! When his tantrums were first ignored, Stephen screamed even louder and longer. It was if he was saying "Can't you hear me? Let me turn up the volume!" It was important for Amy's family to continue ignoring when Stephen did this. They knew that if they gave in to him—even one time—he would learn that all he has to do is scream longer and louder to get what he wants.

Ignoring can be effective, but it can also be difficult. You have to remember that what you *don't* do is as important as what you do. When you ignore, you *don't* talk, touch, answer questions, or look at the person you are ignoring. You do this for as long as they continue to do what you want them to stop doing. If you are ignoring your sister and she tries to climb into your lap or take you by the hand, quietly move away and do something else.

It is also important to reward her for doing what you want her to do. After she quits screaming and crying, say something nice. You might try something like "It's much easier to talk to you when you're not crying." And then pay attention to her.

You can use behavior modification with your sib, parents, friends, teachers, or even yourself. Everyone likes positive reinforcement, even though people are reinforced by different things. What does your sib like? Praise? Hugs? Visits to your room or other special privileges? Use something like this when you want to reward your sib for good behavior. Make it a point to look for good behavior and reward it.

Remember that ignoring is a good technique to use for behaviors like temper tantrums, teasing, and pestering. Be sure to do a good job ignoring, and reward your sib when she acts the right way. Also remember this: if your sibling's behavior is causing you problems that you can't ignore, tell your parents. Your sib's teacher can probably help you set up a more intense behavior modification program for you and your family to try.

A book that can help families set up a behavior modification program is: *Steps to Independence: Skills Training Guide for Parents and Teachers of Children with Special Needs,* by Bruce Baker and Alan Brightman, with Jan Blacher, Louis Heifetz, Stephen Hinshaw, and Diane Murphy, second edition (Baltimore: Paul H. Brookes Publishing Company, 1989). Another book that parents like is: *1-2-3 Magic: Training Your Children to Do What You Want!,* by Thomas W. Phelan (Glen Ellyn, IL: Child Management, Inc., 1995).

Autism

My brother Sam is four years old but he still doesn't talk. Sometimes he'll repeat what you say to him, but most of the time he acts as though he doesn't even hear you. My parents say he has autism.

Autism (ott'-iz-um) is a lifelong *developmental disability* (see page 36) that prevents a person from correctly understanding what he or she sees, hears, or senses. Autism occurs in about 15 out of every 10,000 births. It is usually identified in the child's first three years of life. Autism is four times more common in boys than girls. A person who has autism usually has severe problems learning, communicating, and behaving.

Kids who have autism may have unusual ways of relating to people and objects. They may have very different responses to sound, sight, touch, or pain. Some people with autism are slow in learning to talk. Others do not speak at all, or only repeat what they have heard. People with severe forms of autism may repeat certain actions over and over. However, people with less severe forms of autism may lead normal lives and only differ in the way they relate to other people. One woman who has autism, Temple Grandin, went to college, earned a Ph.D., and wrote about her life in the books *Emergence: Labeled Autistic* and *Thinking in Pictures.*

Doctors think that autism is caused by abnormal (not normal) brain development or brain damage. Although they don't totally understand what causes this damage, they have found that many children with autism were born too early, had other problems at birth, or had infections that hurt the brain. Since these problems can also cause mental retardation (page 33) or cerebral palsy (page 87), a person with autism may also have these conditions. Autism is *not* caused by a child's relationship with his or her parents, or by other psychological or environmental problems.

Most but not all people with autism also have mental retardation. Special education programs that teach children with autism to control their behavior can be helpful for the child and family.

Chapter 4

Disabilities That Children Are Born With

Birth Defects

Many children are born with their disabilities. These disabilities result from a birth defect. A birth defect is a type of problem that is present at the infant's birth. Some birth defects may be caused by problems a child inherits from his parents. These birth defects are called congenital (con-jen'-na-tal) defects. Birth defects can also be caused by something in the environment, such as an infection, or the mother's exposure to certain drugs or chemicals during pregnancy. They can also be caused by a combination of inherited and environmental factors. Many times we don't know what causes a birth defect.

Are there ways to find out if a baby will have a birth defect before it is born?

Ultrasound tests, a blood test called MSAFP (Maternal Serum Alpha Fetoprotein), and amniocentesis can tell doctors a lot about unborn fetuses. (The unborn infant is called a fetus from the time it is eight weeks old until it is born. Before that, it is called an embryo.)

Ultrasound. Ultrasound tests use sound waves to make a picture of the fetus. The sound waves bounce off the fetus's body parts. The waves bounce off hard parts (such as bone) differently than off softer body parts (such as muscles). The ultrasound machine records the different "echoes" of the sound waves as they bounce off the fetus's body parts. The machine then turns the "echoes" into a picture. (This way of making pictures is similar to the way that bats and submarines use sound waves to locate things in the dark.) The pictures made by the ultrasound machine can help doctors diagnose some birth defects before a child is even born. Some of the problems that can be detected with ultrasound are spina bifida (see page 70), hydrocephalus (see page 69), heart problems, and problems with arms and legs. Using ultrasound, doctors can often tell whether the fetus is a boy or a girl!

MSAFP (Maternal Serum Alpha Fetoprotein). MSAFP is a simple blood test that is performed on most pregnant women. It measures the mother's "alpha-fetoprotein." If the mother's alpha-fetoprotein (or AFP) is high, her fetus *may* have spina bifida or other problems. If her AFP is low, her fetus *may* have Down syndrome (page 75). To be certain, the mother will need an amniocentesis.

Amniocentesis. Amniocentesis (am'-nee-o-sen-tee'-sis) is a medical procedure that helps the doctor tell if the fetus has certain birth defects. Amniocentesis also tells the doctor the sex of the unborn child. The procedure gets its name from the amniotic (am'-nee-o'-tic) fluid that surrounds the fetus. This fluid is studied to identify possible problems, like spina bifida, fragile X syndrome, and Down syndrome. Amniocentesis is usually done when the woman is fourteen to seventeen weeks pregnant. The doctor inserts a hollow needle through the mother's belly into the amniotic fluid and takes out a small amount of fluid. This fluid is studied in a laboratory. The fluid contains cells from the developing fetus. These cells are studied for problems that can cause birth defects.

Won't the needle hurt the baby or the mother?

The needle doesn't hurt the mother. While the mother is having an amniocentesis, the doctor uses ultrasound to learn where the baby is. This allows the doctor to put the needle in a place where it will not hurt the baby.

Do all pregnant women have to have amniocentesis?

A doctor may recommend amniocentesis if a pregnant woman is over thirty-

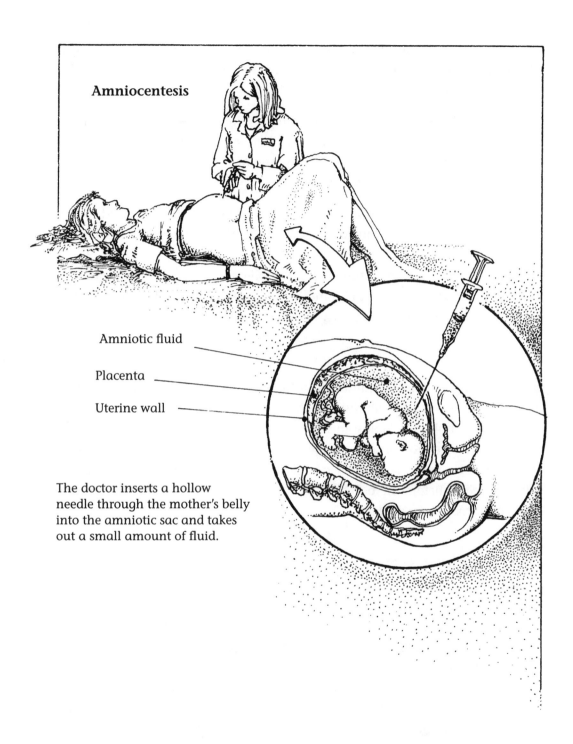

Amniocentesis

Amniotic fluid

Placenta

Uterine wall

The doctor inserts a hollow
needle through the mother's belly
into the amniotic sac and takes
out a small amount of fluid.

The amniotic fluid is studied in a laboratory. The fluid contains cells from the developing fetus. These cells are studied for certain changes that cause birth defects.

Disabilities That Children Are Born With **65**

five years old. This is because a mother's chance of having a baby with a birth defect (such as Down syndrome) increases as she gets older. A doctor may also recommend amniocentesis if:

- she had an MSAFP level that was unusually high or low;
- she has had a previous miscarriage (lost her baby early in pregnancy);
- she has a relative with an inherited disease; or
- she already has a child with a disability.

When amniocentesis reveals that a woman is going to have a child with a severe birth defect or a serious disease, she will receive genetic counseling to help her decide what choices are best for her family.

It's important to remember that not all disabilities can be diagnosed with amniocentesis. Women can have children with disabilities even though they had normal amniocenteses when they were pregnant.

What causes birth defects?

One of the most common questions siblings ask is *why* their baby brother or sister was born with a disability. Sometimes doctors can trace the cause to a change in the baby's chromosomes. Other times, doctors decide it was caused by something the mother was exposed to when she was pregnant. Still other times, doctors determine that the defect was caused by something the father was exposed to before the baby was conceived. *About half of the time, no one knows what caused the disability.*

Birth Defects Caused by Chromosome Changes

The cells in your body have 46 chromosomes, except for the male's sperm cells and female's egg cells. Egg and sperm cells have only 23 chromosomes each. After an egg is fertilized, cells divide and multiply as the baby grows inside the pregnant mother.

Some disabilities occur when the mother's egg cells or the father's sperm cells do not divide in a normal way. This is what happens in most cases of Down syndrome. With Down syndrome, an egg or a sperm cell may have 24 instead of 23 chromosomes. If an egg with 24 chromosomes is fertilized by a sperm with 23 chromosomes, the child will have 47 chromosomes (24+23) instead of the usual 46. If the extra chromosome is a "number 21" chromosome, the child will have Down syndrome or trisomy 21 (see page 75).

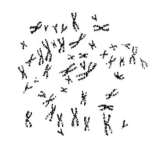

A normal body cell contains 46 chromosomes.

1	2	3	4	5

6	7	8	9	10	11	12

13	14	15	16	17	18

19	20	21	22	23

These are the chromosomes of a child who does not have Down syndrome. The chromosomes are organized and numbered to study.

1	2	3	4	5

6	7	8	9	10	11	12

13	14	15	16	17	18

19	20	21	22	23

These are the chromosomes of a child with Down syndrome. There is an extra chromosome on the 21st pair.

Birth Defects Caused By Things in the Environment (Teratogens)

Some birth defects are caused by a mother's or father's exposure to things in the environment, such as radiation, drugs (including alcohol), infections, and diseases. As a group, these things that harm a growing baby are known as teratogens (te-rat'-e-jens). Teratogens can interfere with the cell division and cell growth of the fetus.

Disabilities That Children Are Born With

Radiation—a teratogen—can cause birth defects. X rays are radiation. That is why a woman should tell her doctor that she might be pregnant before receiving X rays. Certain infections and viruses are also teratogens and can cause birth defects. For example, pregnant women who are exposed to German measles have a high risk of having a child with several birth defects.

Some drugs and chemicals cause birth defects. We now know that women who smoke cigarettes, drink alcohol, or use cocaine while pregnant are more likely to have infants who are born with mental and physical defects.

Fetal Alcohol Syndrome

Fetal alcohol syndrome (FAS) is the leading known cause of mental retardation. It is more common than Down syndrome, fragile X syndrome, and spina bifida. It is also a type of mental retardation that can be prevented. Fetal alcohol syndrome occurs when women drink alcohol while they are pregnant. When a pregnant mother drinks alcohol, so does her developing baby. The alcohol impairs the fetus's cell, brain, and nerve growth. Children who have FAS frequently look different, probably because of the effect alcohol has on cell growth. These children often have small heads, small eyes, no ridge between the nose and the upper lip, and a flat face and nasal bridge. Their development is delayed, especially their language. They usually have problems with behavior, learning, and using good judgment.

Again, FAS is a disability that can be prevented. Doctors know that the more a pregnant mother drinks the greater her chances are that she will have a child with FAS. But they don't know if there is a "safe" level of drinking for pregnant women. That's why doctors advise that women abstain from alcohol during pregnancy.

When a mother is exposed to a teratogen will determine how the infant is affected. Exposure to teratogens early in a pregnancy can result in defects that affect the baby's brain, or the arms and legs. This is because these are the body parts that develop at the beginning of a pregnancy. Exposure during the middle of the mother's pregnancy may affect the child's eyes, and exposure at the end may damage the child's brain or muscles.

Common Birth Defects

*My brother has a birth defect, and so does my friend's sister, but they are
so different. How many kinds of birth defects are there?*

There are many kinds of birth defects. Some are very rare. Below we will discuss some of the more common ones.

Hydrocephalus

The origins of this word are hydro (water) plus cephalus (head). Hydrocephalus (hi-dro-sef'-a-lus) results when fluid builds up in the brain. Normally, fluid circulates between the brain and spinal column. A birth defect, an injury, or an illness may stop the fluid from circulating and cause it to collect in the brain. The fluid accumulates (builds up) in cavities inside the brain called ventricles and presses on the brain cells and nerves. Children with hydrocephalus who

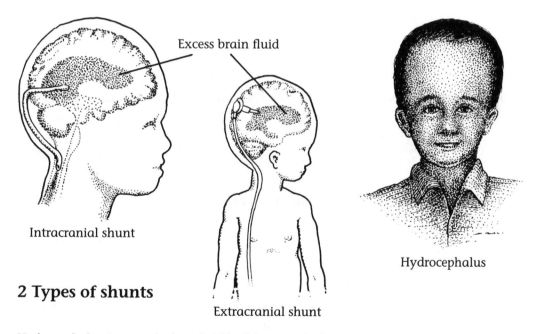

Excess brain fluid

Intracranial shunt

2 Types of shunts

Extracranial shunt

Hydrocephalus

Hydrocephalus is caused when fluid builds up in the brain. Doctors treat it by inserting a shunt, or tube, which drains the fluid into other parts of the body. The intracranial shunt drains excess brain fluid just past the blockage. The extracranial shunt drains excess body fluids to other body cavities.

Disabilities That Children Are Born With   **69**

are not treated may be mentally retarded or paralyzed (unable to move part of their body). Because of the pressure, they may also have seizures (see page 91). Hydrocephalus often occurs in children with spina bifida (see below). It may also result from a head injury, or an infection like meningitis (see page 82).

Hydrocephalus is treated by inserting a small tube, called a shunt, in the child's head. This tube drains the excess fluid from the brain. It prevents fluid and pressure from building up and damaging the brain. Siblings often ask where the water goes when the tube is put in. The tube drains the extra water into other parts of the body, where it will not collect as it does in the brain.

If hydrocephalus is not treated, the fluid will increase the pressure within the infant's head. This pressure will cause the head to expand by pushing open the bones of the infant's soft skull. As the child develops, the bones around the brain harden. When hydrocephalus occurs in an older child, there is no room for the brain to expand inside its hard, bony case. The increased pressure can cause serious problems if the condition is not treated.

Spina Bifida

Spina bifida (spy'-na bi'-fi-da) is a birth defect that is caused when the spinal cord does not develop properly. Spina bifida is Latin for "split spine." Normally, early in the development of the embryo, a layer of cells thickens and forms a groove. By four weeks, this groove closes to form the neural tube, which will become the child's brain and spinal cord. Later, the backbones grow around the neural tube to protect the delicate nerves inside.

Sometimes, for reasons we do not understand, the backbones do not close to protect the spinal cord. Part of the spinal cord or its covering often sticks out from the opening in the backbone. The nerves that go to this open part of the spinal cord don't work the way they should. This may mean that the nerves that send messages to the legs don't work, and the child can't walk without braces or crutches. Some children must use a wheelchair.

The location of the opening on the spinal cord will influence how much spina bifida will affect a child. Usually, when the defect is high on the spinal cord, the disability will be more severe. Here's the reason why: when the spinal cord is open, damage is done to the nerves below the opening. These nerves send signals to other parts of the body. A defect on the lower part of the spinal cord will be less severe because fewer nerves will be affected.

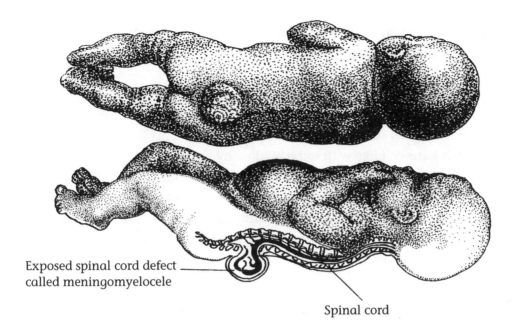

Exposed spinal cord defect
called meningomyelocele

Spinal cord

Spina bifida occurs when the spinal cord does not develop properly and part of the spinal cord is exposed.

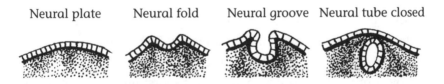

Neural plate   Neural fold   Neural groove   Neural tube closed

Normally, this is how the spinal cord develops and becomes encased in the neural tube, which becomes the child's backbone. The neural tube and later the backbone protect the delicate nerves inside

Some children with spina bifida may have very weak leg muscles or may be completely paralyzed from the waist down. The child's back and feet may change shape when those muscles are not used. Many children with spina bifida do not have complete control of their bowels and bladders. Children who cannot control when they urinate may learn how to insert a small tube into their bladder to empty it.

Children with spina bifida often require many different kinds of treatment. The young infant with spina bifida usually has surgery to close the opening in the spinal column. Another problem that can result from spina bifida is hydrocephalus (see page 69). When hydrocephalus occurs, a shunt, or drainage tube, is often surgically inserted. The shunt drains the fluid from the child's brain to other parts of the body.

Children who are paralyzed may need braces, crutches, or a wheelchair to get around. When the child develops back or foot deformities, or other changes, he or she may need surgery to correct them.

Although some children with spina bifida may have mental retardation, most have normal intelligence. Many will have mild learning disabilities. As they grow up, they will need help to learn how to get around, use the toilet, and become independent. The medical treatments and training that are now available for children with spina bifida will permit many of them to marry and hold jobs when they are adults.

Cleft Lip and Cleft Palate

When a child is born with a cleft lip, the upper lip is split, either on one or both sides of the mouth. When a child is born with a cleft palate (pal'-lat), a groove or cleft runs along the middle of the roof of the mouth. The cleft goes from the front of the mouth (behind the teeth) to the back of the mouth. A child may be born with a cleft lip, a cleft palate, or both. These are relatively common birth defects that occur in about one out of every 750 births.

Siblings often wonder what causes cleft lip and palate. Cleft lip and palate are caused by a problem that occurs during the first ten weeks of pregnancy as the face develops. Usually, as cells divide during that time, tissues grow together to form the child's palate and lips. When these tissues do not move in the right direction, there is an opening where the lip or the palate does not grow together. The cause of these birth defects is often not known. However, doctors think that certain drugs and some infections can prevent the tissues from growing together as they should. Sometimes, cleft lip or palate is a condition that children can inherit from their parents.

Children who are born with cleft lip or palate usually have plastic surgery when they are very young, often before they are two years old. They may have surgery again when they are older to close the cleft and to make it less noticeable.

Some people with cleft lip or palate also have hearing problems. This is because a cleft lip or palate can prevent the middle ear from draining properly.

72

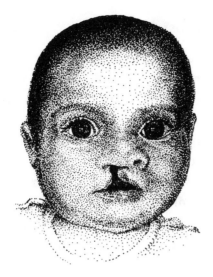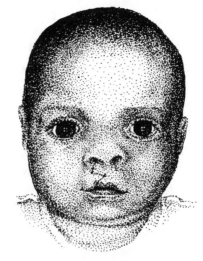

Cleft lip before surgery   Cleft lip repaired at three months

Cleft lip and palate occur when the tissue that forms the lip and palate does not grow together when the baby is developing inside the mother. Both cleft lip and palate can be corrected by surgery. This is a picture of a child with a cleft lip, before and after surgery.

When this happens, the child is more likely to have ear infections. Three out of ten adults born with cleft lip or palate have hearing losses that result from these ear infections. Today, young children with cleft lip or palate may have tiny tubes surgically inserted in their ears. This helps the ear drain and prevents infections that might cause a hearing loss.

If your sib has a cleft lip or palate, you may wonder if he will have other problems as well. Cleft lip or palate is usually an isolated defect—that is, it usually affects only one part of the body. People with a cleft lip or palate are usually not mentally retarded or disabled in other ways.

People with these birth defects usually need the special services of a surgeon, dentist, orthodontist, and speech therapist. These professionals can repair the defect and help the child overcome the speech problems that may result. Stacey Keach, the actor, is an example of a person who had a cleft lip and overcame his speech problems to become a talented stage and movie actor. Also, Blaise Winter, a professional football player who had a cleft lip, volunteers his time as a spokesperson for the Cleft Palate Foundation.

Disabilities That Children Are Born With

Cystic Fibrosis

Cystic fibrosis (sis'-tick fi-bro'-sis) is a disease that causes the lungs and other organs to produce too much mucus. Our bodies normally produce mucus, a thin fluid that helps us breathe and digest our food. Cystic fibrosis causes a person to make too much mucus and mucus that is thick instead of thin. All this thick mucus interferes with the body's normal functions. It can cause bronchitis (an inflammation of the tubes that carry air into and out of the lungs), infections, and lung and heart problems. Children with cystic fibrosis may cough a lot to try to clear their lungs of the extra mucus.

The extra mucus produced by children with cystic fibrosis causes problems for other body parts. The pancreas helps us digest food by releasing enzymes. Too much mucus blocks the release of enzymes.

Brothers and sisters may wonder if there is a cure for cystic fibrosis. Cystic fibrosis is a chronic disease. This means that a person will have it for life. There is no cure for it, but there are many ways that doctors can treat it to make the person feel better. If cystic fibrosis causes lung problems, the child may take medicine for lung infections, or may inhale medicines to keep the lungs cleared. If the pancreas becomes blocked, the child can't get all the necessary nutrients from foods. She will need to take vitamins and other nutritional supplements. Children with cystic fibrosis usually have to eat more than others to get the daily nutrients they need.

Babies are born with "genes" that they get from their mother and father. If you have your father's eyes and your mother's hair, it is because the genes you inherited from your parents directed your body's cells to grow that way. There are many types of genes that cause many types of differences in each person. There is a gene for cystic fibrosis. Children get cystic fibrosis when *both* parents "carry" the cystic fibrosis gene. (The parents don't have the disease; they are just the "carriers" of the gene.)

Doctors may suspect that a baby has cystic fibrosis if she is born with an intestinal blockage. Cystic fibrosis may also be detected when the child is older and develops bronchitis or pneumonia. When doctors discover cystic fibrosis early, they can help children lead longer, better, and more normal lives.

Down Syndrome, or Trisomy 21

Down syndrome is named after the doctor who first wrote about it in medical books, Dr. J. Langdon Down. It is also called trisomy (try'-so-mee) 21, which will be explained below. It is the most common known cause of mental retardation that is identified at birth. More than 7,000 children are born each year with Down syndrome.

A "syndrome" is a group of signs that are commonly found together in a particular condition. There are over fifty signs that may lead a doctor to suspect that a baby has Down syndrome. Some of these signs are floppy muscles, slanted eyes, a single crease across the baby's palm, a nose with a very flat bridge, and very flexible joints. Not all children with Down syndrome will have all of these signs. But they will all have the most important sign: 47 chromosomes.

If you want to understand what causes Down syndrome, you must learn a little about chromosomes. People usually have 46 chromosomes in every cell of their body, except for the male's sperm cells and the female's egg cells. Egg and sperm cells each have 23 chromosomes. Usually, at conception, the 23 chromosomes from the father's sperm cell join with the 23 chromosomes from the mother's egg cell. The fertilized egg, which now contains 46 chromosomes, will divide and grow and eventually become a baby.

Sometimes, for reasons we do not understand, sperm or egg cells divide the wrong way. When they do, the egg or sperm cells end up with *24* chromosomes instead of 23. At conception, then, one parent's 23 chromosomes will combine with the other parent's 24 chromosomes. The fertilized egg will then have a total of 47 instead of 46 chromosomes. The fertilized egg with 47 chromosomes may divide and grow like any other fertilized egg with one big difference: it will have one extra chromosome.

To study chromosomes, scientists have numbered pairs from 1 to 23. Most people have two of each chromosome (two number 1 chromosomes, two number 2 chromosomes, and so on). A person with Down syndrome has three number 21 chromosomes. That's why Down syndrome is also called trisomy (for three) 21. The extra 21st chromosome is responsible for the characteristics seen in children with Down syndrome.

In most cases Down syndrome happens when the sperm or egg cells do not divide properly. In very rare cases a child with Down syndrome will inherit the extra chromosome from a parent who does not have Down syndrome but who is a carrier (see page 74). This is the *translocation* type of Down syndrome and is responsible for about 4 percent of all cases of Down syndrome.

Down syndrome causes some mental retardation. Children with Down syndrome may also have heart and lung problems. They may have hearing and vision problems. Some may have to wear glasses. They may have little tubes inserted into their ears so that fluid does not collect inside their ears and prevent them from hearing.

Some brothers and sisters tell us that they have heard that people with Down syndrome don't live very long. They ask us if that means their brother won't live to grow up and be an adult. In the past, many children with Down syndrome did not live long because of their heart and breathing problems. Today, a child with Down syndrome can have open-heart surgery to repair a heart defect. Children with Down syndrome can take medicine to control infections such as pneumonia (new-mo'-nee-ya) that once were the cause of death.

Sibs often ask us about the special programs and classes their baby brother or sister with Down syndrome attends. In the past, people thought that children with Down syndrome would not be able to learn. Parents of children with Down syndrome were often told to put their babies in institutions—places where the children were raised away from their families. Special education programs for babies, called early intervention programs (see page 106), have helped children with Down syndrome. Because of these programs these babies have learned more than anyone thought possible thirty years ago.

Children with Down syndrome learn many of the things other children learn. It just takes them longer. Everyone in the child's family can share in helping the child with Down syndrome learn to walk, talk, and read. When they are older, persons with Down syndrome may learn to work and live in the community (see Chapter 8, pages 112-16). Adults with Down syndrome may live with other people with special needs or even by themselves if they have help when they need it.

Prader-Willi Syndrome

Like children with other syndromes, children with Prader-Willi (prah'-der wil'-ly) syndrome have certain things in common. When they are babies, they have very floppy muscles. This makes it hard for them to suck and swallow milk like most babies. The baby's mother must often spend many hours trying to feed her child. The child's development is often slow. He may not crawl, sit up, walk, talk, or ride a tricycle until much later than other children his age.

Children with Prader-Willi usually have a serious weight problem by the time they are two or three years old. It is at this time that parents may first find out that their child has the syndrome. Unless the child is on a strict diet, he or she will become very overweight. This can cause serious medical problems when the child grows up. These problems include diabetes, heart disease, and respiratory (breathing) problems.

No one knows for sure what causes Prader-Willi syndrome. Most children with the syndrome have very floppy muscles, are very overweight, and are slower to develop skills than other children. Their faces are alike in some ways too; they often have a triangular-shaped mouth and a narrow face. And they are shorter than other children their age and other members of their family. Some children with this syndrome also have small hands and feet, a curved back, skin problems, and eating problems. About half of all children with Prader-Willi syndrome have mental retardation. Most children with Prader-Willi—even those with mental retardation—can learn to read and do simple arithmetic.

Many children with Prader-Willi syndrome can control their weight if they stay on a very low-calorie and low-protein diet. But this is *very* hard for them to do. When they are put on a diet, they may steal food and have temper tantrums. Many families must lock the refrigerator and the cupboards so that the child cannot sneak food between meals.

The family can help a child who has Prader-Willi by not giving him food that is not on his diet and praising him when he stays on his diet. Sometimes the whole family goes on a diet. They only have food in the house that the child with Prader-Willi can eat. It is important for the family to help the child learn to control how much he eats while he is still young. When he is older and has his own money, the family will not be able to control what he eats. Then the child must be able to use self-control.

It is also important for children with Prader-Willi syndrome to get regular exercise, because this can help them control their weight. Even very young children can get some exercise each day if they ride a tricycle or bicycle. Parents and siblings can help the child with these activities until he is old enough to do them on his own. Older children may jog or do other exercises to control their weight.

As we said, the exact cause of Prader-Willi syndrome is not known. Families who are worried about whether the syndrome is hereditary should see a genetic counselor (see Chapter 8, page 118).

Fragile X Syndrome

Scientists have known for many years that severe mental retardation occurs more often in males than in females, but they did not know why. They now think that fragile X syndrome is the reason.

There is a reason why the syndrome is called "fragile X." When scientists studied the chromosomes of men who have severe mental retardation, they found that many of them had an X chromosome that looks unusual. (X chromosomes and Y chromosomes are called the sex chromosomes. They determine whether we are males or females. Males have an X and a Y chromosome; females have two X chromosomes.) For people who have fragile X syndrome, the bottom of the long arm of the X chromosome looks pinched or fragile.

While both males and females can have fragile X, it affects males the most. Males who have fragile X syndrome often have severe mental retardation and may have behavior problems. They often have long faces, large ears and jaws, and heart problems.

Females who have fragile X often have learning disabilities or mild mental retardation. They also frequently have problems communicating. Their voices may be high-pitched and they may repeat things that others say. They are often shy.

After fetal alcohol syndrome and Down syndrome, fragile X is thought to be the most commonly known cause of mental retardation.

Chapter 5

Other Causes of Disabilities

In Chapter 4, we learned that some children are born with their disabilities. However, some disabilities are caused by things that happen to a child *as* he is being born or *soon after* he is born. These disabilities can be caused by a lack of air, by diseases, or by injuries. They can also be caused by inherited allergies to certain foods, or by an environment that does not stimulate a young child.

My mom says that my sister Jenny's problems were caused because she didn't get enough air when she was born. Aren't some disabilities caused at the time of birth or soon after?

One of the most common causes of disabilities occurs at the time of birth.

Anoxia

Anoxia (an-ox'-ee-a) usually occurs when an infant does not get enough oxygen during birth. The prefix "an" means a lack of, and "oxia" means oxygen, the air we breathe. A loss of oxygen is the major cause of infant deaths at birth.

Some cases of cerebral palsy (see page 87) and mental retardation (see page 33) may be caused by anoxia. Fortunately, most infants who have experienced anoxia do not have any permanent effects. However, a baby's brain can be damaged if she goes without oxygen for too long.

Brain Damage

A person's brain can be hurt, or damaged, *before birth* (see "Birth Defects," page 63). As we just mentioned, brain damage can also happen *during birth* as a result of anoxia. Or it may happen *after birth* as a result of hydrocephalus (page X), automobile accidents, or other head injuries. The brain of a child who has a disease such as encephalitis (an infection that affects the brain) can be hurt. A child's brain can also be damaged by meningitis (page 82) or a very high fever. Brain damage can result in cerebral palsy (page 87), autism (page 61), or epilepsy (page 91). An infant who has brain damage may have mental retardation or may later have trouble paying attention, reading, or writing.

PKU

One inherited food allergy can actually cause mental retardation. It's called PKU. These letters stand for phenylketonuria (fen-al-kee-to-nu'-ree-a). PKU is an inherited condition that can result in mental retardation and other problems. But if PKU is treated in time with a special diet, mental retardation can be prevented.

PKU occurs in about one in 10,000 to 15,000 births and is an "autosomal recessive condition," meaning that the child receives an abnormal gene from each parent. For an infant to be born with PKU, both the mother and the father must be "carriers" of the PKU gene. (They don't have the disease, they just "carry" the gene for it.) When the couple has children, each child has a 25 percent chance of being born with PKU. That is, 25 percent of the time the child will receive two abnormal genes that cause PKU, one from each parent. Two-thirds of the parents' other children will be only carriers for PKU, like their parents.

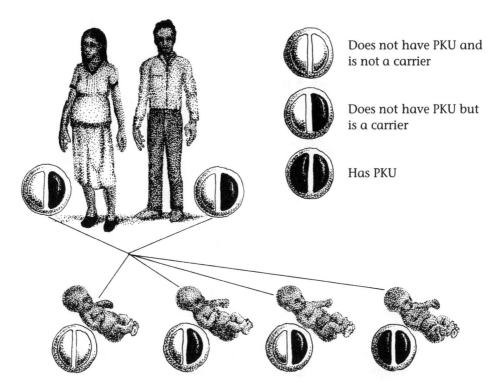

Does not have PKU and is not a carrier

Does not have PKU but is a carrier

Has PKU

PKU is an inherited disorder that can result in mental retardation if it is not detected and treated. PKU is an autosomal recessive condition. This means that it occurs only when the child receives an abnormal gene from each parent.

Children born with PKU are not able to make an enzyme they need to break down an amino acid in the body. (This amino acid is used by the body to help bones, muscles, and internal organs grow.) When this enzyme is *not* present, the amino acid is not broken down and it builds up in the body. Too much of the amino acid can cause mental retardation, behavior disorders, delayed speech, seizures, and muscle problems.

In all states, infants must be tested for PKU shortly after birth. When a blood test shows that the infant has PKU, the child is placed on a special diet. On this diet, the child can't eat foods that are high in protein, such as eggs, milk, cheese, meats, and poultry. She must eat low-protein foods such as fruits, vegetables, and grains. To make sure her diet is complete the child may take a special mixture of vitamins, minerals, and artificial amino acids.

Children may find it harder to stay on this special diet as they get older. They want to eat what their friends eat. Sometimes they become tired of the foods

Other Causes of Disabilities

in their diet. Family and friends can help these children stay on the PKU diet by encouraging them.

Siblings often ask us how long their brother or sister must stay on a special diet. We don't know the answer to that question yet. Some studies show that a woman with PKU who is no longer on a special diet and who becomes pregnant may have a child with mental retardation. Women with PKU who wish to have children may need to stay on the diet until they no longer want to have any more children.

Meningitis

One infection that may hurt a young child's brain and cause permanent disabilities is meningitis (men-in-ji'-tis). Children who have meningitis often have high fevers, stiff necks, and they vomit. They may also have a headache and may have convulsions, which are violent movements of the arms and legs. A case of meningitis looks much like a serious case of the flu, and it usually affects children under the age of five. Unlike the flu, meningitis may have serious permanent effects. The high fever often leads to brain damage and deafness. Meningitis may also cause hydrocephalus (extra fluid in the brain), paralysis (inability to move part of the body), loss of muscle control, and mental retardation. Meningitis may cause cerebral palsy (see page 87) or epilepsy (see page 91) when the infection damages the brain.

Traumatic Brain Injury

Two years ago, Esperanza's older brother, Miguel, was on his way to soccer practice. His bicycle was hit by a car and his head was seriously hurt. He was in the hospital for a long time, but finally he came home and was able to go back to school.

Now Miguel is a senior in high school. Even though he looks completely fine, Miguel has a permanent disability called traumatic brain injury. Before his accident, he used to help Esperanza with her math homework and geography projects. Now

Esperanza helps Miguel with his school work. He has a very hard time remembering his lessons, and it takes him longer to read than it used to. Miguel used to be his soccer team's best forward player. Now he sometimes loses his balance when he climbs the stairs.

Esperanza can see that Miguel is sometimes sad when he thinks about how easy school was for him before his accident. Esperanza and her parents feel sad too. They remember how Miguel used to help everyone in the family with math — he helped Esperanza with her homework, and his parents with the monthly bills. Miguel gets depressed when his friends go off to play soccer together.

Accidents are a major cause of disabilities. Most accidents can be treated and the person completely recovers, but sometimes a child or adult has an accident that results in a permanent disability. For example, a child in a car accident or a sports accident may injure her spinal cord. She may be paralyzed as a result and unable to walk, or talk, or use her hands. A boy who nearly drowns while swimming may have permanent brain damage as a result of his accident.

Accidents are a common cause of disability in adults. Many workers who are injured on their jobs are permanently disabled. Traffic accidents are a major cause of serious disabilities in young male adults. Anyone can have an accident and become disabled.

What is traumatic brain injury?

A major cause of disability in children in this country is traumatic brain injury (TBI). TBI most often happens in car accidents, falls, and sports. More than 1 million children every year have a head injury. Sometimes the brain is injured permanently. A traumatic brain injury may have various effects:

Physical effects. TBI may affect a person's speech, vision, hearing, and other senses. A person with TBI may have severe headaches. She may not be able to use her hands the way she used to. Some people with TBI develop seizures, and some become paralyzed so that they cannot use their legs or one side of their body. A person with TBI may walk with a limp or may lose her balance easily. TBI may affect the person's speech so that he is difficult to understand.

Cognitive effects. TBI may affect the way a person's brain works. For example, a person with TBI may have trouble remembering things she recently learned or things that happened a long time ago. She may not be able to con-

Other Causes of Disabilities 83

centrate on what she is reading. She may have trouble reading or writing, or doing math, like Miguel.

Other effects. When a person has a brain injury, it often affects the way he feels and behaves. Like Miguel, he may be sad and depressed because he cannot do things the way he remembers he could before the injury. Some persons with TBI become moody, and others may get upset very easily.

If the person has a very serious brain injury, the effects may be very severe. If the injury was less serious, there may be only mild effects. After the person with TBI receives assistance from the hospital team and the school, some of these symptoms may lessen. For example, Esperanza's brother has a teacher who started working with him when he was still in the hospital. The teacher helped Miguel learn ways to remember what he learned in his daily lessons. Miguel still needs to organize his work very carefully when he is learning something new. He often needs to practice new skills many times before he is sure he knows them.

With help from teachers, speech therapists, physical and occupational therapists, and other professionals, many persons with TBI, like Miguel, regain some of their previous skills and abilities. But no one can say for sure how a person will recover from a brain injury.

> At first this uncertainty was very hard for everyone in Miguel's family. Now they all understand more about TBI, and the help that Miguel needs to finish high school. Now Miguel's parents and Esperanza know what they can do to make things easier for Miguel. Esperanza's parents tell Miguel how proud they are of his progress in his classes. Esperanza knows how much Miguel misses playing soccer and being at the top of his class in math. When Miguel looks sad, Esperanza invites him to listen to one of her new CDs with her, or they might play a game together. Everyone in the family is learning how to live with the changes in their lives since Miguel's accident.

Child Abuse

Child abuse occurs when someone, most often a parent or another adult, mistreats a child. Often this term is used to mean that the adult hurt the child physically by hitting or beating the child. Child abuse is sometimes called the "battered child syndrome" because abused children may suffer bruises, burns, broken bones, or cuts. Some of these injuries may heal, but others never go away. The greatest danger of child abuse is that the child may receive permanent brain injury.

A parent can also do harm without hitting or striking the child. Neglect is a kind of child abuse that happens when an adult does not give the child enough food, medical care, love, or supervision. Neglect can also have permanent effects on the child's body.

What causes child abuse?

Sibs often ask us why adults abuse children. This is a hard question to answer. Social workers and others who help families of abused children have found that many adults who abuse children were also abused when they were young. Adults who think their children are somehow different from other children are more likely to abuse them. For this reason, infants with disabilities and premature infants can be "at risk" for child abuse. This does not mean that every child born too soon or with a disability will be abused. It only means that these children have a higher than normal chance of being abused.

Child abuse has many causes. Certain things about the child, the parent (or adult), and the particular time and place come together to trigger child abuse. Not all grown-ups who abuse children are bad people. Many times the parent who abuses the child is under a lot of stress. The parent may have had a very unhappy childhood. Some parents who abuse their children do not understand how children develop. They may expect too much of their very young child. When the child can't do what they expect, the parents may get very angry. If the child has a disability, a parent may express his or her disappointment or impatience with the child by abusing him.

Doctors, nurses, social workers, and psychologists are people who often work together to help a family in which there is child abuse. Sometimes the abused child will live with a foster family for a while until the parents get help. Often the person who abused the child will get help from a counselor or will take a class in child development. Other help, such as daycare, financial aid, or homemaking services, may be given to the family. This assistance can relieve the pressures that may have caused the parent to abuse the child. The goal of everyone who works with the family is to protect the child and to keep the family together. If the abuse does not stop, the child will be taken out of the home and put in a safe foster home.

In most states, doctors and teachers must report suspected cases of child abuse to the local child welfare or child protection agency. If you should ever be aware of child abuse, talk to your teacher so that help for the child, the parents, and the family can be given as soon as possible.

Chapter 6

Neurological Problems: Cerebral Palsy and Epilepsy

Your brain, your spinal cord, and the nerves in your body are all part of your nervous system. Your nervous system helps you control and coordinate your movement. It regulates your body's functions and allows your body to respond to stimulation (heat, cold, pain, different textures, sounds, smells, and tastes). Cerebral palsy and epilepsy are called neurological disorders. This is because they affect how the nervous system works, especially how it controls and co-ordinates body movements.

Cerebral Palsy

Cerebral palsy—sometimes called CP—is the name given to any permanent motor (movement) disability that is caused by damage to the developing brain. "Cerebral" refers to the brain. "Palsy" refers to a lack of motor control. CP is a developmental disability, which means it affects how a child grows and learns.

Cerebral palsy results from damage to parts of the brain that control movement. The damage usually occurs before, during, or soon after birth. Doctors say that the damage may happen up to about two years of age. After that age, the brain is so much like an adult's that damage is just called "brain injury" (see page 82). Cerebral palsy may be caused by bleeding in the brain or lack of oxygen in very premature babies. It may also be caused by accidents, maternal diseases, and infections. Sometimes the cause cannot be found.

Cerebral palsy is not a disease. You can't catch it. Once the person's brain is damaged, it does not get any worse. There is no "cure" for cerebral palsy. However, special equipment, therapy, and training can help a person with cerebral palsy control certain movements and communicate needs. Children with CP usually grow up and live adult lives.

Other kids at my brother Carl's school also have cerebral palsy.
Some are in wheelchairs and some can't talk. Others can walk and talk.
Why are they so different?

People who have cerebral palsy are not all the same. Some must use wheelchairs or crutches, while others can walk without help. Some people with cerebral palsy have trouble talking. Some may have to use picture boards or computers to let people know what they need. Others can speak clearly. Sometimes people with CP have vision and hearing problems or have mental retardation. It is important to remember that many people with CP are as smart as anyone else—even though they may have physical disabilities. Christy Brown, who had cerebral palsy, wrote two books about his life (*My Left Foot* and *Down All the Days*), even though he could move only one toe to type.

Are there different types of cerebral palsy? How do they affect a person?

You may hear someone talk about one of the three main types of cerebral palsy: spastic, athetoid, or ataxic. These words describe the kinds of movement problems affecting the person with cerebral palsy.

Spastic Cerebral Palsy

Spastic cerebral palsy makes it hard for a person to move. The movements of a person with spastic cerebral palsy can be very stiff. This is because muscles do not receive the messages the brain sends to make a person move smoothly.

The parts of the body that are affected depend on where the brain was injured. *Hemiplegia* (hem-ee-plee'-gee-ya) occurs when one side of the brain is injured, causing the opposite side of the body to be partly paralyzed. For example, if the left side of a child's brain is injured, the right side of the body will be affected. The child will have *right spastic hemiplegia*. *Quadriplegia* (quad'-ra-plee-gee-ya) occurs when the part of the brain called the cerebral cortex is severely damaged. The person with quadriplegia has spasticity or stiffness in both arms and both legs. If a person has *spastic diplegia* (die-plee'-gee-ya), the legs are affected more than the rest of the body.

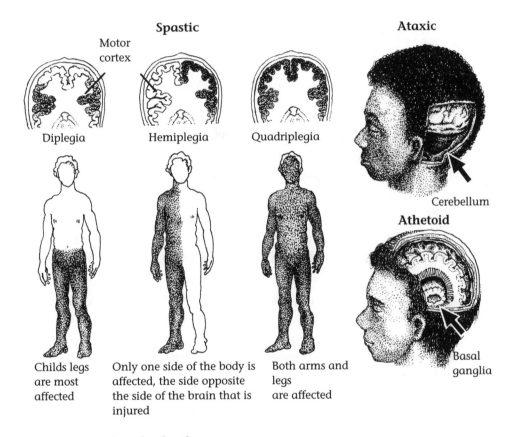

Spastic

Motor cortex

Diplegia

Hemiplegia

Quadriplegia

Ataxic

Cerebellum

Athetoid

Basal ganglia

Childs legs are most affected

Only one side of the body is affected, the side opposite the side of the brain that is injured

Both arms and legs are affected

Different types of cerebral palsy
Cerebral palsy is caused by damage to different parts of the brain.
- Spastic cerebral palsy is caused by damage to the motor cortex or cerebrum. The parts of the body affected will depend on the part of the brain that has been damaged.
- Ataxic cerebral palsy is caused by damage to the cerebellum.
- Athetoid cerebral palsy is caused by an injury to the basal ganglia.

Cerebral Palsy and Epilepsy

Athetoid Cerebral Palsy

You may have heard a doctor say that your sib has athetoid (ath'-a-toyd) cerebral palsy. This causes a person to have involuntary and uncontrolled movements. This form of cerebral palsy is different from spastic cerebral palsy. Spastic cerebral palsy is caused by injury to an area of the brain where movement *originates*. Athetoid cerebral palsy is caused by an injury to the part of the brain that *regulates* movement. Persons with athetoid cerebral palsy have muscles that are sometimes stiff and jerky—like those of a person with spastic cerebral palsy. At other times their muscles are floppy. Because of these shifts in muscle tone, the person with athetoid CP has special problems eating, speaking, sitting, and standing up.

Ataxic Cerebral Palsy

Another kind of CP, called ataxic (a-tax'-ik) cerebral palsy, is caused by damage to the part of the brain called the cerebellum. People with ataxic cerebral palsy (sometimes called ataxia) may have a very poor sense of balance. They may walk the way a drunk person walks. They may not be able to judge distance and may reach farther than they have to when trying to grasp an object.

People with cerebral palsy are being helped by advances in education, medicine, and technology to overcome the effects of their conditions. Organizations such as United Cerebral Palsy (UCP) provide support, information, education, and advocacy (speaking out for people with CP) to persons with cerebral palsy and their families. Most cities have a local UCP center. To find the one in your area, check your local phone book or contact:

United Cerebral Palsy Associations
1522 K Street NW #1112
Washington, DC 20005
Phone: 1-800-872-5827

Physical therapy and occupational therapy (see pages 103 and 105) can help people with cerebral palsy. They can help children who have trouble moving, or using a part of the body, or learning to take care of themselves. Speech therapists (see page 105) can help people with cerebral palsy learn to communicate and eat with fewer problems. Some children, especially those with spastic cerebral palsy, can be helped with special medicines and surgical operations. Braces, wheelchairs, and other special equipment, including computers, can help children with CP to be independent.

Epilepsy

Sally, my little sister, has these spells where she just stops, stares, and drools.
It looks weird, but it doesn't seem to bother her. My mom says she has epilepsy.
I thought people who have epilepsy fall down. Are there different kinds?
What causes it?

Epilepsy (ep'-il-ep-see) is a disorder of the central nervous system that causes repeated seizures. A person who has a seizure temporarily loses control over certain parts of the body. Seizures happen to people with many different diseases, but more often to people with epilepsy.

Seizures

Seizures happen when the brain cells are abnormally active. The brain contains about one hundred billion nerve cells, or neurons. These cells normally send messages to the rest of the body through chemical and electrical signals. Seizures are caused when the neurons send *too much* electrical energy through parts of the brain that control how we move, feel, or sense things. The brain is *not* damaged when a person has a seizure. After the seizure is over, the brain returns to normal.

Most of the time we do not know why a person has seizures. Sometimes siblings ask us whether something they did caused their brother or sister to have a seizure. You cannot cause a person to have a seizure.

There are two major categories of seizures. *Generalized seizures* affect both hemispheres of the brain. *Partial seizures* are limited to a part of one hemisphere.

Generalized Seizures. Most people think of a *tonic-clonic* (or grand mal) seizure when they think of epilepsy. These seizures involve the entire body. Like all generalized seizures, they affect both hemispheres of the brain. Before the seizure begins, the person may have an *aura*, a funny feeling that a seizure is about to happen. Next, the person may pass out and fall to the floor. He may have very irregular breathing, and may even stop breathing for a moment. His body will stiffen, his teeth will clench, and his whole body will begin to jerk. He may bite his tongue or lose control of his bladder and wet himself. Seizures usually do not last more than two minutes. When the seizure is over, the person may feel tired and confused, sometimes for as long as several hours.

A child who has an *absence seizure* may stare, blink, or twitch and be unaware of people or things around him. These seizures usually last less than ten seconds. The child may not remember having the seizure when it is over. These seizures can be hard to recognize because the child may seem to be daydreaming or just not paying attention.

Partial Seizures. Another kind of seizure, called the *partial simple seizure*, begins with a twitching in one part of the body, like the thumb or toe. The seizure gradually spreads to other body parts. During the partial simple seizure, unlike absence and tonic-clonic seizures, the person will usually remain aware of his surroundings. In some cases, the seizure may spread and become a grand mal seizure, and the person may lose consciousness. Like all partial seizures, this type only affects one of the brain's hemispheres.

A *partial complex seizure* is more common in teenagers and adults than in young children. The person may initially smell, taste, hear, or see things that are not there. He may appear to be in a daze or a trance. He will make certain movements, like smacking his lips, chewing, or scratching or tugging at his clothes. He may perspire, become pale, salivate (the mouth will produce a lot of saliva), or get very pink. These seizures last only a minute or two. Afterward, the person may be confused and may not remember what happened.

What causes epilepsy?

Epilepsy, the condition that causes seizures, has many different causes. Head injuries, birth defects, poisons, brain tumors, anoxia (see page 79), and certain infections (see page 82) may damage the brain's electrical system and cause seizures. In about half the cases, the cause is unknown. Some families have a history of epilepsy. If a parent has epilepsy, his or her child has an increased risk of having seizures. But, doctors tell us, parents with epilepsy most often have children who do *not* have it.

How is epilepsy treated?

Most often, epilepsy is controlled with a medicine or combination of medicines. Often the doctor must try out several different medicines to find the kind and amount that will control the seizures and have the fewest side effects. "Side effects" are effects that the medicine has besides controlling the seizures. Depending on the medicine such effects might be sleepiness, swollen gums, an upset stomach, or rashes.

Children with epilepsy that is being controlled with medicine can do just about everything that children without epilepsy can do. Of the people whose seizures are treated with medicine, about half will have their seizures completely controlled, and 30 percent will have fewer seizures. For about 20 percent, the medicine will not help the seizures. Sometimes a special diet can prevent seizures that result from vitamin deficiencies. In some cases, surgery can help people with partial complex seizures.

Epilepsy is often diagnosed in children with cerebral palsy or mental retardation. Most people who have epilepsy have normal intelligence and lead normal lives. Famous people in history who have had epilepsy include James Madison and Thomas Jefferson, early American presidents. Neil Young, the rock star, has epilepsy and has talked about it in interviews.

If you or your family would like more information about epilepsy you should write to:

Epilepsy Foundation of America
4351 Garden City Drive
Landover, Maryland 20785-2267
Phone: 1-800-332-1000

Chapter 7

Laws, Programs, and Services for Persons with Disabilities and Their Families

*My mom and dad go to these meetings at my brother's school with other
parents who have kids with problems like my brother's. They say they learn
about special programs and laws for people with disabilities.
What special programs are there for disabled people?
Why do they need special laws?*

Many children with disabilities will need some kind of special education and special services when they are growing up. This kind of assistance will help the children make the most of their abilities. A law that was passed in 1975 makes it possible for all children with disabilities to get the school programs that meet their needs.

The laws that we talk about in this chapter, like the Americans with Disabilities Act (ADA) and the Individuals with Disabilities Education Act (IDEA) were passed to stop many years of discrimination against persons with disabilities. You have probably studied about different forms of discrimination—the unfair treatment of a person because of race or sex. The Civil Rights Act of 1964 was passed to stop discrimination against people because of their race. But it also protects people from being treated unfairly because of sex, age, religion, and other differences.

The ADA and the IDEA help assure that people with disabilities have the same opportunities for education and employment as people without disabilities. The laws respond to decades of unfair *stereotypes* of persons with disabilities. For example, one stereotype is that persons with disabilities won't be helped by going to school. Another stereotype is that people with disabilities who have a job won't do good work.

Siblings and families of persons with disabilities know that these are not fair ways of thinking about someone who is disabled. Because of this, parents and siblings of persons with disabilities often become advocates for people with disabilities. Advocates speak out about the rights of people with disabilities. Over the years, advocates have worked hard to make sure that people with disabilities get services they need. They have worked hard so people with disabilities can live, work, and play in the community, just like everyone else. They have worked hard to pass laws that let students and workers with disabilities live their lives without being limited by stereotypes.

The Americans with Disabilities Act tells employers that people with disabilities must have an equal opportunity to get a real job. The ADA tells public service providers that people with disabilities must have opportunities to use the bus or train or telephone, just like everyone else in our country. Now, more employers are learning that many people with disabilities can do jobs just as well as people who do not have disabilities.

Before these laws were passed, many children with disabilities did not have the right to go to school to learn! When the law to educate children with disabilities was passed, special programs were created to help children with disabilities learn. Over the years the law was expanded to help preschool children and infants with disabilities.

Advocates worked hard to make these programs and services available to people with special needs. They opened up the doors to opportunities that most people who don't have disabilities take for granted.

The Americans with Disabilities Act

The Americans with Disabilities Act (ADA) is the world's first civil rights law protecting people with disabilities. It was signed into law by President George Bush on July 26, 1990. The ADA was written to make sure that people with disabilities can have the same rights as everyone else. It is an important law that helps people with disabilities lead full lives in their communities.

Who does the ADA help?

To enforce the law, the ADA had to define "Americans with Disabilities." Here is what the law considers an American with a disability:

People with disabilities. The ADA protects people who are limited in one or more of these "major life activities":

- breathing
- seeing
- hearing
- speaking
- walking
- learning
- working and
- caring for oneself

This means that anyone—including your brother or sister—who has problems with any of these "major life activities" now has a civil rights law to protect them! The law also protects people who have AIDS or are HIV positive.

People who *used* to have a disability. The ADA also protects people who are treated differently because they *used* to have a disability. For instance:

> Margaret wanted a job in Richard's bookstore. Richard knows that Margaret once had cancer and was very sick. Richard doesn't want to hire Margaret, because he is afraid that she will get sick again. The ADA prevents people like Richard from refusing to give someone a job just because of his fears about cancer.

People who are *thought of* as having a disability. Leah's story is an example of this.

> Leah is 17 years old and gets good grades. When she was 10, Leah was in a bad fire and has scars on her arms and part of her face. Last week, Leah applied for a job at a fast-food restaurant. She wants to earn money for college. The manager, Ms. Quan, doesn't want to hire Leah. Ms. Quan thinks that Leah can't do the job because of her scars. But the truth is, Leah's scars don't affect her ability to do the job! Ms. Quan is treating Leah as if she had a disability. Under the ADA, it's illegal for Ms. Quan to refuse to hire Leah simply because of her burn scars.

How does the ADA help people with disabilities?

Under the ADA, people with disabilities cannot be segregated (kept away) from people who do not have disabilities. The ADA also makes it illegal to exclude people with disabilities from opportunities that other people have. The law applies to employers, business owners, state and local governments, hotels, and schools.

Because of the ADA, people with disabilities now have rights in the following areas:

Jobs. Now employers can't deny a qualified person a job just because she has a disability. Applying for a job, being hired and fired, getting a promotion or a raise, and job training are all protected by the ADA.

The law also says that employers with 25 or more employees must make "reasonable accommodations" for employees who have disabilities. This means that an employer can't refuse to spend money or make certain changes that make it possible for a qualified person with a disability to work for him. The courts may decide what is a "reasonable" amount of money that an employer can afford.

The ADA requires "accommodations" to make it possible for people with disabilities to be employed. Accommodations are often inexpensive and easy to make. They might include:

- a speech synthesizer that reads print from a computer screen;
- software that makes print on a computer screen larger;

- computers that print in Braille;
- interpreters for workers with hearing impairments;
- flexible work hours for employees who must use limited public transportation (such as buses with wheelchair lifts);
- a mouthstick that allows a person with cerebral palsy to use a computer; or
- a small platform that raises a desk so a person in a wheelchair can use it.

Public Services. Much of the ADA helps people with disabilities with jobs. However, the ADA also helps people with special needs use public services. These services—transportation, restaurants, hotels, theaters, stores, offices, museums, stadiums, schools, and parks—must become accessible to people with disabilities. For instance, public bus and train systems must now buy only buses and trains that can be used by people with disabilities.

The spirit of ADA is opening doors for many people with disabilities, such as Cynthia. Blind since birth, Cynthia was able to "see" a play at a theater that tries to follow the ADA. During the play, Cynthia wore special headphones and listened to someone describe the action of the play as it was performed. This theater also offers performances interpreted in sign language for people who have hearing impairments.

Communications. The ADA also makes it possible for people who can't hear or talk to use the telephone to communicate with people who *can* hear and talk. Here's how it works:

> Anita, who works at a bank, is deaf. She needs to call David, who can hear. To communicate with David, Anita types a message on her TDD. (A TDD—Telecommunication Device for the Deaf—can send written messages over the phone.) Anita's TDD message goes to a special telephone operator. The operator reads the message on her TDD and reads the message to David. The operator can also use her TDD to type David's reply to Anita.

The Americans with Disabilities Act is a very important law. It is similar to the Civil Rights Act of 1964, which says that people should get equal treatment regardless of their race, color, sex, national origin, or religion. Like the Civil Rights Act, the ADA protects the independence and freedom of choice for people with disabilities. It gives them a chance to live fully and equally in our society. It also reminds the rest of us how much people with disabilities *can* do when given a chance!

The Individuals with Disabilities Education Act

In 1975, a federal law—Public Law 94-142—was passed. PL 94-142 made sure that children with disabilities could attend school to get the special education and other services that they needed. Over the years, this law was revised to make the law clearer and help children more. In 1990, the law was revised again and its name was changed to IDEA, the Individuals with Disabilities Education Act.

What does the IDEA do?

IDEA made sure that all children with disabilities could get a "free and appropriate public education." This means that special education and other related services (see below) must be provided for free, and at the public expense.

Who does the IDEA help?

IDEA helps children who have one or more of the disabilities listed below:

- mental retardation
- hearing impairments
- speech or language impairments
- visual impairments
- serious emotional disturbances
- orthopedic impairments
- autism
- traumatic brain injury
- specific learning disabilities
- deaf blindness
- multiple disabilities
- and other health impairments

According to IDEA, children and people up to 21 years of age will get the educational services they need. The law also says that in many states very young children—from birth to age five—can also receive services.

> LaTashia's 27-year-old brother Leonard has mild mental retardation. In 1975, Leonard was in one of the first groups of students who were eligible to receive special education under the federal law. The meant that when he was seven he was placed in a special classroom. He was taught by a teacher trained to teach students who had difficulty learning in the regular classroom.

What is special education?

Special education under IDEA is teaching that is specially designed to meet the needs of a child with disabilities. It can include:

- classroom instruction in regular classrooms
- instruction in a special education classroom or school
- instruction in a resource room in the school
- home instruction
- even instruction in a hospital

The law says that a child's special education must be provided in the least restrictive environment. This means that whenever it is possible and appropriate, a child with disabilities should receive her education in the regular classroom.

IDEA also makes sure that children with disabilities receive related services when they need them. Related services include things like:

- occupational therapy
- physical therapy
- speech pathology
- transportation to educational services
- audiology services

> Hernando's sister, Alicia, has Down syndrome. At her school, a special education teacher works with her for part of the day in the regular classroom. Alicia also receives speech therapy to improve the way she articulates her words.

The kind of special education that a child receives is determined by the child's IEP, or Individualized Education Program.

Jim has a seven-year-old brother, Dave, who has mental retardation. Unlike Leonard in the example above, Dave is more likely to get his special education in the regular classroom. IDEA makes sure that children with disabilities get the special education that is appropriate to the child's needs. Now, in the 1990s, we know more about how to teach children with disabilities. Teachers know more about how to teach these children in the same room as their classmates who do not have special needs.

How do children with disabilities get special education services?

The first step in receiving special education is being tested by school staff who are specially trained. The information from these tests is reviewed by a team of school staff. This team includes someone who is an expert in the child's special area of need, like mental retardation or learning disabilities.

If the child is found to be eligible for special education, school staff meet with the child's parents. The purpose of this meeting is to develop an Individualized Education Program.

How does the Individualized Education Program work?

An IEP is a written plan for an education program that will meet a child's special needs. An IEP describes:

- the child's learning goals, and
- the services the school will provide to meet those goals.

The IEP also includes the following information:

- the child's current educational level,
- yearly goals for the child's education,
- services provided to meet those goals, and
- how much regular education the child will receive.

Parents help write their child's IEP and continue to review it during the year.

What happens if parents disagree with the school's decisions about their child?

The IDEA includes many *procedural safeguards*. This means that there are ways of protecting a child's and family's rights. The safeguards describe ways of settling disagreements about a child's education.

Examples of procedural safeguards written into the laws include:

- the right of parents to see and review their child's education records,
- the right to request a special meeting if the parents disagree with school officials,
- the privacy of the child's school records.

> Jerryl's parents, Mr. and Mrs. Waters, did not agree with the school's placement of his sister. The school wanted to place Linda in a special education classroom. Mr. and Mrs. Waters requested a "due process hearing." At the hearing Mr. and Mrs. Waters said why they thought that Linda would do better in a regular classroom with special help. A hearing officer listened to Linda's parents and the school officials. The officer also reviewed other information, such as test scores, to make a decision about where Linda would go to school.

Why does the law for special education keep changing?

Special education laws are always changing to keep up with the current best thinking about special education. For example, in 1990, the law expanded the definition of special education. The new definition includes teaching in the workplace and in training centers for older students who have disabilities.

Physical Therapy

I know that kids with cerebral palsy need to go to physical therapy and occupational therapy, but I don't know what they do there. What is the difference between PT and OT? Do they hurt?

If your sibling has difficulty sitting, crawling, or walking, he may receive physical therapy (PT). Children who have cerebral palsy, Down syndrome, juvenile arthritis, spina bifida, or who have been in accidents often need help from a physical therapist. Your sib may get his PT in school, at a clinic or a hospital, or at home. A physical therapist is someone who is trained to help people move easier and get stronger.

Physical therapists who work with young children choose special activities, games, and exercises to help them stretch their arms and legs and build stronger muscles. For example, if a baby cannot lift her head, the physical therapist may use a toy. The PT will move the toy to encourage her to look up and lift her head. If a child's arms or legs are weak or stiff, the therapist may pick special exercises so the child will learn new movements. The therapist will also teach the family the special exercises so that the child can get lots of practice at home.

A physical therapist helps children who are slow to develop certain skills or need to overcome the effects of physical disabilities.

If a child needs braces, crutches, or a wheelchair, a physical therapist will help her learn how to use them properly.

Siblings have asked us whether physical therapy hurts. Sometimes the stretching may hurt a little. However, when the child practices the exercises and stretches his muscles, the exercises will become familiar and not hurt.

Occupational Therapy

An occupational therapist (OT) is someone who can help a child who has difficulty eating, dressing, bathing, playing, or using the toilet. Like the physical therapist, the occupational therapist may work with a child at school, in a clinic, or at home. If a baby has difficulty eating or feeding himself, an occupational therapist may develop a program for the family to use at home during mealtime. The program may be exercises to make the child's tongue and jaw stronger. Or the program might include using special spoons or plates to make it easier for the child to scoop his food.

Speech and Language Therapy

Children who have problems with their speech, language, or hearing (see pages 43-50) may work with a speech therapist. Like other therapies, speech therapy may be offered in a clinic, at home, or in the classroom. Speech therapists help children who stutter or have difficulty pronouncing words. They often give advice to parents and teachers on how to get children with language problems to talk more and express themselves better. Speech therapists also help children communicate using sign language (see page 47), boards, or even computers.

Some children with cerebral palsy or other problems have a hard time making their mouth, tongue, and lips work together to eat or make words. Some speech therapists work with children to control their mouth, tongue, and lips so they can eat better and talk more clearly. Often speech therapists teach parents what they can do at home to help their child.

Laws, Programs, and Services

Early Intervention Programs

Does your baby brother or sister have a disability? Do your parents worry because your baby sib isn't doing what babies her age should be doing? If so, your baby brother or sister may need an early intervention program. Early intervention programs are for babies who are just a few months old to about three years old. They are also called infant education programs, stimulation programs, or early education programs. In a way, they are like schools for babies.

What can a baby learn in school?

You might not think that babies can go to school. People used to think that babies could not do very much, let alone learn things. In fact, not very long ago

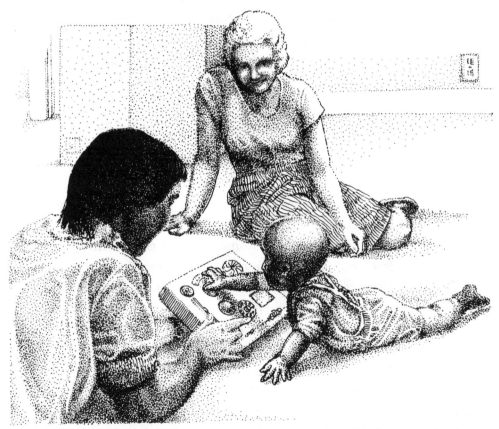

Parents go to school with their baby so they can learn how to help their baby learn at home.

106

many people thought that babies could not even see or hear very well. But when psychologists and others began to study babies, they discovered that babies are pretty smart and are learning all the time! Babies can see and hear quite well when they are born. They practice using their eyes when they play with their parents. They learn to connect sounds with the things that make sounds, like bells or rattles. They also learn to connect sounds with the people who make them, like the funny voice a big brother uses when he plays with his baby sister. They learn to use their hands to reach for things they see and hear, like a bottle, a rattle, or a sister's ponytail. Most of the things babies learn, they learn when they are playing. That way, learning happens all the time as the baby grows.

If babies learn by playing, why do they have to go to school?

When a baby has a disability, he or she is not always able to learn the same things that other babies learn just by playing. For example, Rosie is a baby who does not have a disability. Rosie began to learn to crawl when she saw a toy that she liked at the other end of the room. She would also try to crawl when her mother stretched out her arms and called to her. A baby with vision or hearing problems may not be able to see or hear the things that made Rosie want to crawl. This is when early intervention programs can help. If a baby cannot see, the teacher can help the baby listen for sounds that the baby finds interesting. Then, she will help the baby find the source of the sound. The teacher can help the baby move her arms and legs to crawl and find a music box or a ball with bells inside.

Infant programs are different from kindergarten or first grade. Most often, the baby's mother or father goes to school with the baby. This way, they learn how to help the baby at home. In some early intervention programs, the baby doesn't go to school, the school goes to the baby! With "home-based" early intervention programs, teachers bring toys and equipment to a child's home or daycare.

It's really important that early intervention programs work with parents and others who care for a baby with special needs. This is because babies are at home most of the time, and they learn mostly by playing with their parents. At the early intervention program, parents may learn games and exercises that they can play with their babies. These activities can help babies learn to sit up, roll over, walk, drink from a cup, or play with other children. Parents who learn these activities can teach others in the family how to help the baby when they are playing, feeding, or dressing her.

If your baby sib goes to an early intervention program, you may want to visit the program. Your sib's teacher can explain what she does with your baby sib, and how you can help!

Respite Care

It's really hard for our family to do things together. My brother's behavior problems make it hard for us to take him anywhere. They also make it hard to find a baby-sitter for him. My parents say they are trying to get some "respite care" for Sam. What is respite care?

A respite (ress'-pit) is a rest. Respite care gives the family a break from caring for a child with a disability. The rest may be very short—maybe just a few hours, long enough for the parents to go out to dinner or a movie. It may be longer, like a week or two, so the whole family can take a vacation together without the child with special needs. During this respite, a person who knows about the child's disability will take care of the child so the family does not have to worry. This person may be specially trained or have experience caring for a family member with a disability.

Respite can be very hard to plan when a child has many special needs. If a child has severe disabilities, someone must always look after the child, and the family never has a chance to do things together. Families may not be able to hire a neighborhood baby-sitter to look after the child with the disability. Most baby-sitters would not know how to care for the child's many needs. As a result, parents may never get to go to a movie together. Families may give up vacation plans. Parents and the other kids in the family may miss out on times that help families feel close.

This is why respite care is so important. It allows family members time to have some fun together. It can help families avoid getting "burnt out" from caring for the child with special needs.

The sad news is that respite care is sometimes hard to find. In many cities,

108

Respite care gives a family some time off from caring for the child with special needs.

parents cannot find someone who they can trust to care for their child with special needs. Or, when trained respite care providers are available, they are often very expensive. Some states have respite care programs. These states pay people to give respite care to families with children who have special needs. We think families should get respite care when they need it—both in emergencies and when families need to take a break and go away together.

If you want to find out about respite care in your community, call your local Arc. They should be listed in your phone book. (If not, call their national office at 1-800-433-5255.) Someone at the Arc should know if there are people who offer respite care in your area. If there aren't, you may want to ask them what it would take to start a respite care program in your town. In some cities, Easter Seals societies or United Cerebral Palsy programs offer respite care for families.

Laws, Programs, and Services

Chapter 8

The Future

Thinking about the future can make you feel both excited and worried. It can be exciting to daydream about growing up, having an interesting job, traveling, being independent, and having a family. On the other hand, thinking about the future can also be scary. Will you find a job you like? Will you earn enough money to buy all your food and a house? You may ask yourself a lot of questions when you think about the future, like "Who will I marry?" "Where will I live?" "How many children will I have?" "What will I be?"

Brothers and sisters of children with special needs also think about the future. However, they may also have a few questions that other siblings *don't* have. They may wonder:

- What's going to happen to my sibling with special needs when she grows up?
- Where will my sib live?
- Will I have to take care of my sib when my parents get older or die?
- Will I have a baby who has a disability like my brother's?

For many sibs these are tough questions that are hard to talk about with parents. The answers will depend on your sib's disability, your family's beliefs, and your community's resources. Here are some ideas to help you get the answers that will match your needs.

When Sibs with Disabilities Grow Up

Where will my sister live when she grows up?

To live on our own, away from our parents, is a normal desire for adults in our country. People with disabilities often have this desire too. It is normal to expect that your brother or sister will someday live away from home. However, finding a good place for a person with a disability to live can be hard. Where your sib will live will depend on your sib's disability, her preferences, your family's desires, and the resources available in your community. Here is a sampling of types of places where adults with disabilities live.

Family Care

Some adults with disabilities continue to live at home with their parents or brothers and sisters. But this can become difficult for parents as they grow older, especially if their child needs a lot of assistance in everyday tasks. It can also be difficult for brothers and sisters, especially if they have their own children to raise.

Adult Family Homes

Many states provide adult family homes for people with disabilities. These are private homes where someone is able to take good care of the adult with special needs. The state licenses these adult family homes to make sure they are safe and caring places.

Group Homes

Many states have group homes for people with disabilities. A group home often has four to ten adults who live together. Group homes are often located in a neighborhood and near community services, like a shopping area, a park, and a community center. In large cities, there is likely to be a group home that is near to the family of the disabled person.

Group homes are supervised by people who are trained to take care of the people who live there. For example, the supervisor in a group home for adults who are blind needs to know about the special needs of persons who cannot see. Adults who live in group homes often go to school or work at a job. The adults who live in a group home also often have chores—cleaning their room or helping cook dinner—to help take care of the home. They often take part in community activities, like playing baseball or swimming at the local pool.

Supported Living

If your sibling is able to do many things for himself, he may live in an apartment or a home. He may live alone or with one or several roommates. If he needs help, someone who is trained may help him with the things he is not able to do himself. This helper may live in the same building or may live nearby. These are some examples of supported living:

Sam's sister, Julie, is 25 and has cerebral palsy. She has lived alone for two years in an apartment. She is able to do many things for herself, but she needs help with some of her housecleaning.

Sandy's brother, Tim, is 30 and has Down syndrome. Tim lives in a house with his housemates who also have special needs, Luis, Mike, and Doug. They share many of the housekeeping chores and like to go bowling together. An independent-living instructor checks on them every day to make sure that things are running smoothly and to help them when help is needed.

Kim's sister Tina is 22 and is blind. She lives in an apartment with Susan, a roommate who does not have a disability. Tina and Susan usually have dinner together and both like music and walks in the park. Susan helps Tina with the bills and with transportation to places she cannot get to on the bus.

Most people with disabilities who live in supported housing have jobs and use other community services, such as buses, the library, and neighborhood shopping areas.

The kind of community housing that is available for persons with disabilities varies. Some states have more programs than others, and some cities have better programs than others. You can find out what is available in your state from your local Arc. To get the address of the Arc in your community, check your phone book, contact the United Way, or write:

The Arc
500 East Border Street
Suite 300
Arlington, Texas 76010
Phone: 1-800-433-5255

It's important to remember that where your sibling lives and works will probably change, just as your living place and job will change over time. Just like you, she may learn skills so she can move to a new home or job. She will always be able to take advantage of new living or job opportunities that come up in the future.

Where will my brother work when he grows up?

The kind of job that your sibling will have will depend on his disability and the job programs available in your community. Many children with disabilities now begin to prepare for their future employment while they are still in high school, and even earlier. The goal is to find a job that will best use all the person's abilities.

Sheltered Employment

Jason's sister, Sharon, is blind and has mental retardation. Since last September she has worked in a sheltered workshop. She sorts pieces of telephone equipment into bags and counts the number of pieces per bag. She is paid for the numbers of bags that she completes per week.

Sheltered workshops are helpful for training people with disabilities to get ready for regular jobs in the community. At a workshop, people with disabilities learn skills that are important to be successful. These skills might be getting to work on time, working hard, and getting along with other workers. Some sheltered sites are located within a local industry. The workers with disabilities are trained and get used to working in an actual work site. Workers trained in these sites are helped to move into independent jobs.

Some people with severe disabilities may never have the skills to hold a competitive job. These people may stay in a sheltered job and continue to receive support. The pay a person gets in a sheltered workshop is often based on their ability to produce.

Supported Employment

Jalessa's brother, Jamal, has mild mental retardation. Last month Jamal began work in a supported employment program. Recently he learned to take the bus to meet his job coach at a downtown hotel. Jamal is learning how to be a bellman and carry bags. His job coach, Vic, is helping Jamal learn the many parts of his job. Vic is also helping him work with the other hotel workers and visitors. Vic says that soon Jamal will be working on his own without any help.

Whenever possible, a goal for a person with a disability is to work in a regular job. In supported employment, a person with a disability works one-on-one with a job coach to take a job in the community. Along with the training, the workers with disabilities may get other kinds of support, such as transportation. Some workers will continue to get support to make sure that they are doing well in their work and are being treated fairly. Other workers, like Jamal, go on to work independently.

There are many benefits to supported employment. Workers earn money they can use to pay rent, buy food, and go to the movies. This helps them live more independently. Workers often receive insurance and retirement benefits. They have a chance to get to know people who do not have disabilities. Often, they can advance in their job as they learn new job skills.

Maria, who is blind, had been looking for a good job for almost a year. Recently she got a job as a receptionist with a large company. Using a special computer and an adapted phone, she is able to handle the many important calls her company receives. Her hard work has been praised by the president of the company, as well as the company's customers.

Competitive Employment

Passage of the Americans with Disabilities Act (ADA) (see page 97) provided

"What will happen when my sib grows up? Will I have to take care of him when my parents are no longer around?"

protection for workers with disabilities. The ADA makes sure that they have the same opportunities for independence as anyone else. Because of the ADA, a person with a disability who is qualified for a job cannot be discriminated against because of his or her disability.

A counselor may help a person with a disability find and prepare for a competitive job. The counselor may help the person get training and learn the job-seeking skills needed to compete for a job opening. Later, the counselor may help the person advance in her job and meet the social demands of the work setting.

You can see that people with disabilities have many choices about where they will live and work when they grow up. Your family will probably start to talk about these choices as your sibling grows up. Join in these discussions! Brothers and sisters often have very good ideas. These discussions will help answer some of your questions about the future.

Caring for a Grown-up Sibling

There is one question that many siblings have that is difficult to ask parents. When you think about growing up and getting married you may wonder: Will I have to take care of my sibling with special needs when my parents are no longer around? The answer to this tough question is very simple: you will have only those responsibilities that you want. There are state programs and agencies that will take care of your sib. The staff are trained to make decisions for him when needed. Many people, however, want to make sure that their sibs live in the best possible place. They want to make sure that their sibs have a good job and enough of the little "plusses" that make life enjoyable. They want to have a say in the lives of their brothers and sisters.

There are legal ways to make sure that you can have a voice in your sib's life when you grow up—if that is what you want. You will need to talk to your parents about your part in your sibling's future. It is *their* responsibility to make sure that your brother or sister will be cared for when they are no longer around. Ask your parents if they have any plans for your sibling's future. If they haven't, let them know that you are thinking about your future and your sib's future. Show them this book.

Some families set aside money in wills or trusts for their special child's future. When some siblings grow up, they decide they want to become the legal guardian for their brother or sister with special needs. A legal guardian makes important decisions for another person. To become a legal guardian, you must go to court. Your local Arc can give you and your family more information about how to plan for your special sib's future.

Worries about Your Own Future

Will I have a baby with a disability like my sibling's?

The answer to this question depends on the type of disability your sibling has. If the disability is the result of an accident during or after birth, your chance of having a healthy baby is as good as anyone's. If your sibling was born with a disability, there is a chance that his condition can be passed on to your children. *The chances depend on the disability*. Doctors we talked to say that if you are unsure if your sib's disability is hereditary, you should ask your parents. You and your parents may wish to visit a genetics clinic and ask them. Genetics clinics are often located at state university medical schools and at large hospitals. A phone call to your doctor or to a nearby hospital can help you find a genetics clinic in your area. Also, you can contact your local March of Dimes office. If you can't find your local office, contact:

March of Dimes
1275 Mamaroneck Avenue
White Plains, New York 10605
Phone: 914-428-7100

It is important that you and your brothers and sisters understand your chances of having children with a hereditary disability. This is information your parents or your doctor, school nurse, or counselor can help you obtain.

Conclusion

It was hard to stop writing this book! There are so many questions we wanted to answer for brothers and sisters, but couldn't. If we did, this book would be so long you wouldn't want to read it! Some sibs may still want information about disabilities that aren't included in these pages. Others may have questions about special medical treatments. If you would like to learn more about a disability, illness, treatment, or service, here are some things you can do:

- Ask your parents. This is often a great place to start. You'd be surprised at what parents know! Sibs tell us that the best time to ask parents questions is when you are alone with them. Try the quiet time just before going to bed. Or in the car, on the way to basketball practice. If you don't feel good about asking your parents, think about asking another adult. A favorite aunt, uncle, grandparent, or other trusted adult can often provide you with helpful information.
- If you have questions that you think your sibling's doctor, nurse, or teacher could answer, ask them! Ask your parents if you can go to your sibling's next clinic visit or IEP meeting. Your parents should let them know you are coming and tell them that you have questions for them.
- Read all about it. On the pages that follow are names of organizations that

help people with special needs and their families. Write them a letter like this:

> Dear friend:
> My brother has (name of disability). I am ___ years old. Do you have information for kids about (name of disability)? If so, please send me a copy. If not, would you please write something just for kids?
> Thank you,
> (your name)
> (your address, zip code, and phone number)

- Tell us! You are holding the second edition of *Living with a Brother or Sister with Special Needs*. For the second edition, we added new sections on attention deficit disorder, fragile X, and other disabilities because brothers and sisters asked us to do so.

We've enjoyed writing this book and we hope you have enjoyed reading it. At the very end of this book are some questions. Please write your answers and mail them back to us. We want you to tell us if you liked the book and how we could make it better.

Please take care, and write us! We think brothers and sisters are the greatest!

Appendix 1

Books for Young Readers about
Disabilities and Illnesses

(recommended reader ages are given in parentheses)

Autism

Bodenheimer, C. 1979. *Everybody Is a Person: A Book for Brothers and Sisters of Autistic Kids.* Syracuse, NY: Jowonio/The Learning Place. (11-14)

Gold, P. 1976. *Please Don't Say Hello.* New York: Human Sciences Press. (8-13)

Parker, R. 1974. *He's Your Brother.* Nashville, TN: Thomas Nelson. (11-15)

Spence, E. 1977. *The Devil Hole.* New York: Lothrop, Lee and Shepard. (11-14)

Werlin, N. 1994. *Are You Alone on Purpose?* New York: Houghton Mifflin. (14-17)

Blindness and Visual Disabilities

Eyerly, J. 1981. *The Seeing Summer.* Philadelphia: J. B. Lippincott. (8-12)

Hall, L. 1982. *Half the Battle.* New York: Charles Scribner's Sons. (11-15)

Kent, D. 1979. *Belonging.* New York: Ace Books. (11-15)

Little, J. 1972. *From Anna.* New York: Harper and Row. (11-16)

Little, J. 1977. *Listen for the Singing.* New York: E. P. Dutton. (11-16)

McPhee, R. 1981. *Tom and Bear.* New York: Thomas Y. Crowell. (9-15)

Marcus, R. 1981. *Being Blind.* Mamaroneck, NY: Hastings House. (10-15)

Weiss, M. E. 1980. *Blindness.* New York: Franklin Watts. (11-14)

Wolf, B. 1976. *Connie's New Eyes.* New York: Harper and Row. (11-15)

Cancer

Amadeo, D. M. 1989. *There's a Little Bit of Me in Jamey.* Morton Grove, IL: Albert Whitman and Co. (8-13)

Murray, G., and G. Jampolsky, eds. 1983. *Straight from the Siblings: Another Look at the Rainbow.* Berkeley, CA: Celestial Arts. (8-18)

Cerebral Palsy

Emmert, M. 1989. *I'm the Big Sister Now.* Morton Grove, IL: Albert Whitman and Co. (7-11)

Fassler, J. 1975. *Howie Helps Himself.* Morton Grove, IL: Albert Whitman and Co. (3-7)

Little, J. 1962. *Mine for Keeps.* Boston: Little, Brown and Co. (8-12)

McPhee, R. 1981. *Tom and Bear.* New York: Thomas Y. Crowell. (9-15)

Metzger, L. 1992. *Barry's Sister*. New York: Atheneum Macmillan. (9-17)

Nolan, C. 1987. *Under the Eye of the Clock*. New York: St. Martin's Press. (14 and up)

Perske, R. 1986. *Don't Stop the Music*. Nashville, TN: Abingdon Press. (11-14)

Rabe, B. 1981. *The Balancing Girl*. New York: E. P. Dutton. (4-7)

Slepian, J. 1980. *The Alfred Summer*. New York: Macmillan. (11-17)

Southall, I. 1968. *Let the Balloon Go*. New York: St. Martin's Press. (9-15)

Cystic Fibrosis

Arnold, K. 1982. *Anna Joins In*. Nashville, TN: Abingdon Press. (4-8)

Deafness and Hearing Problems

Hlibok, B. 1981. *Silent Dancer*. New York: Messner. (3-6)

Hyman, J. 1980. *Deafness*. New York: Franklin Watts. (11-15)

Peterson, J. 1977. *I Have a Sister, My Sister Is Deaf*. New York: Harper and Row. (11-13)

Walker, L. 1985. *Amy: The Story of a Deaf Child*. New York: E. P. Dutton. (7-13)

Diabetes

Kipnis, L., and S. Adler. 1979. *You Can't Catch Diabetes from a Friend*. Gainesville, FL: Triad Scientific Publishers. (6-14)

Emotional and Behavioral Problems
Attention Deficit Disorder

Gehert, J. 1992. *I'm Somebody Too.* Fairport, NY: Verbal Images Press. (9-17)

Moss, D. 1989. *Shelley, the Hyperactive Turtle.* Rockville, MD: Woodbine House. (4-8)

Epilepsy

Epilepsy Foundation of America. 1992. *Brothers and Sisters: Just for You!* Landover, MD: Author. (7 through adult)

Hermes, P. 1980. *What If They Knew?* New York: Harcourt Brace Jovanovich. (11-14)

Herzig, A., and J. L. Mali. 1982. *A Season of Secrets.* Boston: Little, Brown and Co. (11-17)

Moss, D. 1989. *Lee, the Rabbit with Epilepsy.* Rockville, MD: Woodbine House. (4-8)

Learning Disabilities

Evans, S. 1986. *Don't Look at Me.* Portland, OR: Multnomah Press. (7-11)

Little, J. 1968. *Take Wing.* Boston: Little, Brown and Co. (11-14)

Pevsner, S. 1977. *Keep Stompin' Till the Music Stops.* New York: Seabury. (11-15)

Smith, D. B. 1975. *Kelly's Creek.* New York: Harper and Row. (11-15)

Mental Retardation
(includes Down syndrome)

Baldwin, A. N. 1978. *A Little Time*. New York: Viking Press. (9-15)

Bradbury, B. 1970. *Nancy and Her Johnny O*. New York: Ives Washburn, Inc. (14 and up)

Byars, B. 1970. *The Summer of the Swans*. New York: Viking Press. (11-15)

Cairo, S. 1985. *Our Brother Has Down's Syndrome: An Introduction for Children*. Toronto, Ontario, Canada: Annick Press Ltd. (4-11)

Cleaver, V. 1973. *Me Too*. Philadelphia: J. B. Lippincott, Inc. (11-15)

Dodds, B. 1993. *My Sister Annie*. Honesdale, PA: Caroline House Boyds Mills Press. (11-15)

Edwards, J., and D. Dawson. 1983. *My Friend David*. Portland, OR: Ednick Communications. (14 and up)

Friis-Baastad, B. 1967. *Don't Take Teddy*. Charles Scribner's Sons. (11-14)

Gillham, B. 1981. *My Brother Barry*. London: Andre Duetsch Ltd. (10-13)

Hansen, M. 1985. *Straight from the Heart*. Saskatoon, Saskatchewan, Canada: Saskatchewan Association for the Mentally Retarded. (12-17)

Hesse, K. 1991. *Wish on a Unicorn*. New York: Henry Holt and Co. (9-16)

Hirsch, K. 1977. *My Sister*. Minneapolis, MN: Carolrhoda Books. (5-8)

Konschuh, S. 1991. *My Sister*. Calgary, Alberta, Canada: Paperworks Press Ltd. (3-8)

Laird, E. 1989. *Loving Ben*. New York: Delacorte Press. (11-17)

Lasker, J. 1974. *He's My Brother*. Morton Grove, IL: Albert Whitman and Co. (3-7)

Litchfield, A. 1984. *Making Room for Uncle Joe*. Morton Grove, IL: Albert Whitman and Co. (6-9)

Little, J. 1968. *Take Wing*. Boston: Little, Brown, and Co. (10-13)

Lynch, M. 1979. *Mary Fran and Mo*. New York: St. Martin's Press. (14 and up)

Miner, J. C. 1982. *She's My Sister: Having a Retarded Sister*. Mankato, MN: Crestwood House. (11-14)

Nolette, C. D., T. Lynch, S. Mitby, and D. Seyfreid. 1985. *Having a Brother Like David*. Minneapolis, MN: Children's Medical Center. (7-11)

Perske, R. 1984. *Show Me No Mercy*. Nashville, TN: Abingdon Press. (14 and up)

Reynolds, P. 1968. *A Different Kind of Sister*. New York: Lothrop, Lee and Shepard. (10-14)

Rodowsky, C. 1976. *What About Me?* New York: Franklin Watts. (14 and up)

Shyer, M. 1981. *Welcome Home, Jellybean*. New York: Scribner. (11-15)

Slepian, J. 1990. *Risk n' Roses*. New York: Philomel Books. (9-16)

Smith, L. B. 1977. *A Special Kind of Sister*. New York: Holt, Rinehart, and Winston. (5-8)

Sobol, H. 1977. *My Brother Steven Is Retarded*. New York: Macmillan. (5-8)

Thompson, M. 1992. *My Brother, Matthew*. Rockville, MD: Woodbine House. (7-11)

Welch, S. K. 1990. *Don't Call Me Marda*. Wayne, PA: Our Child Press. (8-16)

Wright, B. R. 1981. *My Sister Is Different*. Milwaukee, WI: Raintree Children's Books. (7-12)

Physical Disabilities

Berger, G. 1979. *Physical Disabilities*. New York: Franklin Watts. (11-15)

Greenfield, E., and A. Revis. 1981. *Alesia*. New York: Philomel. (11-14)

Muldoon, K. M. 1989. *Princess Pooh*. Morton Grove, IL: Albert Whitman and Co. (7-13)

Rosenberg, M. B. 1983. *My Friend Leslie*. New York: Lothrop, Lee and Shepard. (5-8)

Siegel, I. M. 1991. *Everybody's Different, Nobody's Perfect*. Tucson, AZ: Muscular Dystrophy Association. (7-11)

Schizophrenia

Knoll, V. 1992. *My Sister Then and Now*. Minneapolis, MN: Carolrhoda Books. (7 and up)

Sibling Loss

Hickman, M. W. 1984. *Last Week My Brother Anthony Died*. Nashville, TN: Abington Press. (4-8).

LaTour, K. 1983. *For Those Who Live*. Omaha, NE: Centering Corp. (13-18)

Spina Bifida

White, P. 1978. *Janet at School*. New York: Crowell. (3-5)

General Books About Disabilities

Adams, B. 1979. *Like It Is: Facts and Feelings about Handicaps from Kids Who Know*. New York: Walker and Co. (8-12)

Brown, T. 1982. *Someone Special Just Like You*. New York: Holt, Rinehart and Winston. (3-7)

Kamlen, J. 1979. *What If You Couldn't? A Book about Special Needs*. New York: Charles Scribner's Sons. (11-16)

Lobato, D. J. 1990. *Brothers, Sisters, and Special Needs: Information and Activities for Helping Young Siblings of Children with Chronic Illnesses and Developmental Disabilities*. Baltimore: Paul H. Brookes Publishing Co. (adult)

McConnell, N. P. 1982. *Different and Alike*. Colorado Springs, CO: Current, Inc. (11-15)

Meyer, D. J., and P. F. Vadasy. 1994. *Sibshops: Workshops for Siblings of Children with Special Needs*. Baltimore: Paul H. Brookes Publishing Co. (adult)

Rosenberg, M. 1988. *Finding a Way: Living with Exceptional Brothers and Sisters*. New York: Lothrop, Lee and Shepard. (7-14)

Schwier, K. M. 1992. *Keith Edward's Different Day*. San Luis Obispo, CA: Impact Pubs. (7-11)

Appendix 2

Organizations and Other Resources on Specific Disabilities and Illnesses

AIDS

CDC National AIDS Clearinghouse
P.O. Box 6003
Rockville, Maryland 20849-6003

National Pediatric HIV
Resource Center
15 South Ninth Street
Newark, New Jersey 07107

Attention Deficit Disorder

Attention Deficit Information Network
475 Hillside Avenue
Needham, Massachusetts 02194

Children and Adults with
Attention Deficit Disorders
499 NW 70th Avenue, Suite 109
Plantation, Florida 33317

Autism

Autism Society of America
7910 Woodmont Avenue, Suite 650
Bethesda, Maryland 20814

Center for Study of Autism
9725 SW Beaverton-Hillsdale
Highway, Suite 230
Beaverton, Oregon 97005

Blindness and Visual Impairments

American Council of The Blind
1155 15th Street Northwest, Suite 720
Washington, D.C. 20005

American Foundation for the
Blind, Inc.
15 West 16th Street
New York, New York 10011

National Association
for the Visually Handicapped
22 West 21st Street, Sixth Floor
New York, New York 10010

Cancer

Candlelighters Childhood
Cancer Foundation
7910 Woodmont Avenue, Suite 460
Bethesda, Maryland 20814

National Cancer
Information Service
Office of Cancer Communcations
Building 31, Room 10A16
31 Center Drive, MSC 2580
Bethesda, Maryland 20892

Cerebral Palsy

United Cerebral Palsy Association, Inc.
1660 L. Street Northwest, Suite 700
Washington, D.C. 20036

Cleft Palate

American Cleft Palate Cranio-Facial Association
1218 Grandview Avenue
Pittsburgh, Pennsylvania 15211

Cystic Fibrosis

Cystic Fibrosis Foundation
6931 Arlington Road
Bethesda, Maryland 20814

Deafness and Hearing Impairments

National Association of the Deaf
814 Thayer Avenue
Silver Spring, Maryland 20910

Alexander Graham Bell Association
3417 Volta Place Northwest
Washington, D.C. 20007

Diabetes

American Diabetes Association
National Service Center
1660 Duke Street
Alexandria, Virginia

Juvenile Diabetes Foundation
International
432 Park Avenue South, 16th Floor
New York, New York 10016

Down Syndrome

National Down Syndrome Congress
1605 Chantilly Drive, Suite 250
Atlanta, Georgia 30324

National Down Syndrome Society
666 Broadway, Eighth Floor
New York, New York 10012

Emotional and Behavioral Disorders

Federation of Families for Children's
Mental Health
1021 Prince Street
Alexandria, Virginia 22314

National Mental Health Association
1021 Prince Street
Alexandria, Virginia 22314

National Alliance for the Mentally Ill
200 North Glebe Road, Suite 1015
Arlington, Virginia 22203

Epilepsy

Epilepsy Foundation of America
4351 Garden City Drive
Landover, Maryland 20785

American Epilepsy Society
638 Prospect Street
Hartford, Connecticut 06104

Fetal Alcohol Syndrome

Family Empowerment Network:
Support for Families
Affected by FAS/FAE
610 Langdon Street, Room 521
Madison, Wisconsin 53703

National Organization on Fetal
Alcohol Syndrome
1815 H Street NW
Washington, DC 20006

Fragile X Syndrome

FRAXA Research Foundation
P.O. Box 935
West Newbury, MA 01985

National Fragile X Foundation
1441 York Street, Suite 215
Denver, Colorado 80206

Fragile X Association of America
P.O. Box 39
Parkridge, IL 60068

Genetic Diseases

March of Dimes Birth Defects Foundation
1275 Mamaroneck Avenue
White Plains, New York 10605

Head Injury

National Head Injury Foundation, Inc.
1776 Massachusetts Avenue Northwest, Suite 100
Washington, D.C. 20036

Hydrocephalus

Hydrocephalus Association
870 Market Street, Suite 955
San Francisco, California 94102

National Hydrocephalus Foundation
22427 South River Road
Joliet, Illinois 60436

Learning Disabilities

Learning Disabilities Association of
America, Inc.
4156 Library Road
Pittsburgh, Pennsylvania 15234

The Orton Dyslexia Society
Chester Building, Suite 382
8600 LaSalle Road
Baltimore, Maryland 21286

National Center for Learning Disabilities
381 Park Avenue S., Suite 1420
New York, New York 10016

Mental Retardation

The Arc
500 East Border Street
Arlington, Texas 76010

American Association on
Mental Retardation
444 North Capitol Street NW
Suite 846
Washington, D.C. 20001

Prader-Willi Syndrome

Prader-Willi Syndrome Association
2510 S. Brentwood Boulevard, Suite 220
St. Louis, Missouri 63144

Spina Bifida

Spina Bifida Association of America
4590 MacArthur Boulevard NW,
Suite 250
Washington, D.C. 20007

Tay-Sachs Disease

National Tay-Sachs and Allied
Diseases Association
2001 Beacon Street, Suite 204
Brookline, Massachusetts 02146

Tuberous Sclerosis

National Tuberous Sclerosis Association, Inc.
8181 Professional Place, Suite 110
Landover, Maryland 20785

Other Syndromes

Tourette Syndrome Association
42-40 Bell Boulevard
Bayside, New York 11361

Cornelia de Lange Syndrome
Association
60 Dyer Avenue
Collinsville, Connecticut 06022

Williams Syndrome Association
P.O. Box 297
Clawson, Michigan 48017

International Rett Syndrome
Association
9121 Piscataway Road, Suite 2B
Clinton, Maryland 20735

Turner's Syndrome Society
Twelve Oaks Center
15500 Wayzata Boulevard
Building 768, Suite 214
Wayzata, Minnesota 55391-1416

National Marfan Syndrome
Foundation
382 Main Street
Port Washington, New York 11050

Support Organizations for
Trisomy 18, 13, and Related
Disorders (SOFT)
2982 South Union Street
Rochester, New York 14624

Sources of General Information on Disabilities

National Information Center
for Children and Youths
with Disabilities
P.O. Box 1492
Washington, D.C. 20013

Direct Link for the disAbled
P.O. Box 1036
Solvang, California 93464

Index

Index   139

Sibling Feedback Form

Brothers and sisters! Please use this page and tell us what you think about this book. (If this is a library book, don't write on this page! Photocopy the Sibling Feedback Form or copy your answers on another sheet of paper.) We'll use this information to make the next edition of *Living with a Brother or Sister with Special Needs* even better.

Date:_____

Age: _____

Your name: _____

Address and zip code: _____

The name of your sibling with special needs: _____

Is there a name for your sibling's disability or illness? If so, please write it here:

_____

☐ I don't know the name of my sibling's special needs.

What were your *favorite* parts of *Living with a Brother or Sister with Special Needs*?

What were your *least favorite* parts of *Living with a Brother or Sister with Special Needs?*

Were there parts of the book that were hard to understand?

If you wrote a book for brothers and sisters, what would you include?

Is there anything else you would like to tell us about our book or about being the sibling of a person with special needs?

Thank you for your thoughts! Please mail the Sibling Feedback Form to:

Donald Meyer
Sibling Support Project
Children's Hospital and Medical Center
P.O. Box 5371, CL-09
Seattle, Washington, 98105-0371